HIGHLAND DANCING

HIGHLAND DANCING

The official textbook of
The Scottish Official Board of Highland Dancing

THOMAS NELSON AND SONS LTD
LONDON EDINBURGH PARIS MELBOURNE
TORONTO AND NEW YORK

THOMAS NELSON AND SONS LTD
Parkside Works Edinburgh 9
36 Park Street London W1
312 Flinders Street Melbourne C1
218 Grand Parade Centre   Cape Town

Thomas Nelson and Sons (Canada) Ltd
91–93 Wellington Street West   Toronto 1

Thomas Nelson and Sons
19 East 47th Street New York 17

Société Française d'Editions Nelson
25 rue Henri Barbusse Paris V^e

———

First published 1955

THE SCOTTISH OFFICIAL BOARD
OF HIGHLAND DANCING

OFFICE-BEARERS

President	The Most Honourable the Marquess of Huntly
Vice-President	Brigadier Alasdair G. L. Maclean, C.B.E., of Pennycross
Chairman	Mr Harry Fairley
Secretary	Miss Catherine Collie (actg.)
Treasurer	Mr J. S. Thompson

DELEGATES

Dance Associations

British Association of Teachers of Dancing	Miss M. F. Lindsay	Mr J. Turpie
British Ballet Organisation	Miss A. Calder	Miss K. Garland
British Ballet Organisation (Australasian Branch)	Miss A. Calder	Miss B. Jessiman
Highland Dance Specialists' Association	Miss C. Tucker	Mr T. Reid
North British Ballrooms Associations	Mrs I. Macdonald	Mr J. F. Stewart
Royal Scottish Country Dance Society	The Lord James Stewart Murray	Captain J. Bain
Scottish Dance Teachers' Alliance	Miss C. Robertson	Mr J. Muir
United Kingdom Alliance of Professional Teachers of Dancing	Mrs J. Ferguson	Miss P. MacDonald

Her Majesty's Forces

The Army	Major P. W. Forbes	Major H. Hall

Games Associations

Cowal Highland Gathering	Mr J. S. Thompson

Piping Associations

Highland Pipers' Society	Miss J. Reynolds	Dr A. C. McLaren

INDEPENDENT MEMBERS

Major A. A. Bourne, Brigadier H. J. D. Clark, Mr R. M. Cuthbertson, Miss J. H. Lindsay, Brigadier A. G. L. Maclean, Mr J. L. McKenzie, Miss N. Ross, Miss J. Stewart, Miss E. P. Wallace, Mr R. Watson, Captain T. S. Davidson (*Honorary*).

ACKNOWLEDGMENTS

Gratitude is due especially to the following members of the Board, who have rendered invaluable service : Miss Jean J. C. McLellan, who was for two years one of the S.D.T.A. delegates, and who carried out the secretarial duties during the formation of the Board ; Captain T. S. Davidson, who succeeded Miss McLellan in the Secretaryship and carried it on until forced, for reasons of health, to resign ; and Mr D. G. McLellan, whose co-operation we still happily enjoy.

Valuable services have also been rendered by the following former Delegates and Independent Members : Miss M. Brown, Miss B. Findlay, Colonel A. Gordon, Miss M. F. Hadden, Mrs P. Keay, Miss J McLellan, Mr D. G. McLennan, Dr A. Robertson, Mr B. Robertson, Major A. D. Rowan Hamilton, Miss A. Stewart, Mr. R. Thomson.

NOTE ON ILLUSTRATIONS

The occasional lack of sharpness in the reproduction of plates numbered 39–70 is due to the fact that they are stills taken from a moving colour film. This film, 'Highland Dancing, Basic Positions and Basic Movements', is the official film on Highland Dancing of the S.O.B.H.D.

CONTENTS

CONTENTS

INTRODUCTION

In any particular country the evolution of a national form of dancing is bound to give rise to diverse opinions as to the correct method of performing that country's traditional dances unless it is controlled by some one generally recognised authority. Many of the innovations which have periodically appeared in Highland Dancing were accepted by dancers all over Scotland, but certain brilliant exponents of the art have, from time to time, introduced new ideas and variations of their own. These new ideas were adopted only by the pupils and followers of those who invented them, and there has developed a chaotic situation, in which our traditional dances are danced differently in different parts of our country. Dancers competing at the various games throughout Scotland have had to vary their style and alter their steps according to the district in which they were competing, or according to the known stylistic preferences of the judges before whom they were appearing.

Various associations of teachers, and many individuals well versed in Highland Dancing, have compiled their own descriptions of our traditional dances, and their own versions of the traditional technique. Some of these accounts of Highland Dancing resemble one another fairly closely, but no two of them are exactly alike.

To the organisers of Highland Games, that part of the programme which was concerned with Highland Dancing was a constant thorn in the flesh. Complaints were continually being made to them about bad or biased judging, or about unsatisfactory features in the conduct of the competitions ; and there is no doubt that an appreciable percentage of those complaints was justified. Yet the organisers could do little or nothing about them, because there was no generally recognised authority to which they could refer such complaints for consideration and necessary action. Nor was there any body to which competitors having a legitimate grievance against the organisers of, or the judges at, any particular Games could appeal, because the rules laid down by the promoters of any particular competition were not applicable to other competitions, and there were no generally applicable rules governing the conduct of championships or other competitions of lesser importance. Furthermore, there being no rules to give a clear definition of the status of the amateur dancer, the term ' amateur ', in most instances, was merely farcical.

Towards the end of the year 1949 the Scottish Dance Teachers' Alliance made a move towards bringing this unsatisfactory state of affairs to an end, by advocating the establishment of a representative board of control. The principal aims and objects of the board would be to stabilise the technique of Highland Dancing, to formulate laws and regulations covering every aspect of the art, and to do everything in its power to further the interests of our national dancing. It was fitting that this first move should have been made by the Alliance, because it is the only association of professional teachers of dancing which can, by reason of its constitution, claim to be purely Scottish. Getting in touch with other associations which foster Highland Dancing, and with various organisations which sponsor Highland Games, the Alliance invited each of these bodies to send delegates to a meeting specially convened for the purpose of considering the advisability of establishing a representative body to control Highland Dancing. Many prominent personalities, well known to the public as exponents (past or present), as judges, or as patrons, of Highland Dancing, but not connected with any professional association, were also invited to attend this meeting. Mr James Adam having kindly offered, for this purpose, the Plaza Ballroom in Stirling, the meeting took place there in January 1950. It was presided over by Mr Jack Muir, who was President of the Alliance at that time, and resulted in the inauguration of ' The Scottish Official Board of Highland Dancing '.

This Board is representative of all organisations and individuals interested in any aspect of Highland Dancing, and its constitution makes provision for : four Office-Bearers ; two delegates each from Represented Members (Scottish Associations or those with Scottish branches) and Affiliated Members (Overseas Associations) ; one delegate each from a limited number of Games Organisations ; and not more than ten Independent Members.

This book sets forth the stabilised technique of Highland Dancing which has been compiled by the Board and adopted by all associations and individuals connected with that body. This is tantamount to stating that practically every qualified teacher of Highland Dancing in Scotland has adopted that technique. The book also contains rules and regulations, formulated by the Board, pertaining to our national dancing in all its other aspects.[1]

In every part of the world where Scots are to be found, and particularly in every part of the British Commonwealth, there is usually a Scottish Society of some description, and most of these societies are sponsors of Highland Dancing. As ambassadors for this branch of our national culture they look, naturally, to their mother country for guidance, as is shown by the amount of correspondence received by the Board from overseas. Hitherto they have been in a quandary as to whose description of the Highland dances, and whose version of the technique, they should adopt. Now, with the advent of the Scottish Official Board of Highland Dancing, they have available to them authoritative, practical and comprehensive instructions governing that art in all its aspects. Moreover, if they wish further advice or clarification of any point on which they are in doubt, they need only communicate their difficulty to the Board, which will be very happy to render them every assistance in its power.

[1] Originally it was intended also to provide a brief but authoritative account of the history of Highland Dancing. Gradually, however, it became clear that the difficulties in the way of such an attempt are at present well-nigh insuperable : reliable evidence concerning origins and early development is scarce and scattered ; in the general neglect of Scottish culture which has prevailed, until recently, in all four Scottish universities, Highland Dancing has been largely ignored by learned men ; and as yet little or no serious research has been done. There is an opportunity here for academic investigators which, it is to be hoped, they will not fail much longer to exploit.

Chapter One

BASIC POSITIONS AND BASIC MOVEMENTS

General Remarks and Preliminary Definitions

1 The body should be held in a natural easy manner without stiffness, strain or exaggeration.

2 The foot supporting the weight of the body is called the SUPPORTING FOOT. The other foot is called the WORKING FOOT. While dancing, it is always the ball of the Supporting Foot that is in contact with the ground.

3 It should be the aim of the dancer to keep the supporting leg turned out at an angle of $45°$ to the Line of Direction (see p. 5), and the working leg turned out at an angle of not less than $45°$—and in many cases $90°$—to the Line of Direction. This turning out of the knees tends to keep the apron of the kilt flat.

4 When executing any movement of elevation, the dancer should land on the count except where otherwise stated.

5 When the working foot has to be placed in or raised to any specified position whilst executing a movement of elevation, that foot arrives at the specified position simultaneously with the dancer landing on the supporting foot, unless otherwise stated.

6 (*a*) BASIC POSITIONS are the essential positions of the feet, arms and head on which all movements are founded.
(*b*) A BASIC MOVEMENT is the combining, by movement, of two or more Basic Positions.
(*c*) A BASIC STEP is a combination of Basic Movements.

§*A. BASIC POSITIONS*

1 FOOT POSITIONS

In this book foot positions are described and illustrated as nearly as possible as they should appear in actual dancing.

Definitions

A CLOSED POSITION is one in which the feet are either in contact with each other, or the working foot is touching the supporting leg. (An exception is Third Crossed Position.)

An OPEN POSITION is one in which the working foot is not in contact with the supporting foot or the supporting leg.

A GROUND POSITION is one in which both feet are in contact with the ground.

An AERIAL POSITION is one in which the working foot is off the ground.

A REAR POSITION is one in which the working foot is to the rear of the supporting foot.

Preliminary Remarks

There are five *basic ground positions* of the feet, namely, First Position, Second Position, Third Position, Fourth Position and Fifth Position. In addition to these there are three *derived positions* : one, being a variation of Third Position is called ' Third Crossed Position ' ; the other two, both variations of Fourth Position, are called ' Fourth Intermediate Position ' and ' Fourth-opposite-Fifth Position '.

In a *ground position* the following terms are used in describing various methods of placing the working foot.

(a) *Toe.* When in contact with the ground, without pressure, in an open position with the instep arched, or in a closed position with the foot vertical, it is said to be *pointed* or placed on the *toe*. When the working foot is pointed in an open position the knee of the working leg is kept straight.

(b) *Half point.* When the pads of the first two or three toes are in contact with the ground, with the ball of the foot off the ground, it is said to be placed on the *half point*.

When placed on the half point in an open position, the instep of the working foot should be arched with the knee of the working leg slightly relaxed ; in a closed position, the working foot should be kept as vertical as possible.

When the working foot is placed on the half point, the weight of the body is partially taken on it ; the main weight is retained on the other foot, thus providing the impetus for the slight elevation or travel of that (i.e. the supporting) foot during the half point.

(c) *Ball.* When the pads of the toes and the ball of the foot are in contact with the ground with the instep arched, it is said to be placed on the *ball*, and the knee of the working leg is kept as straight as possible, but *without strain*, to allow for freedom of movement.

When the working foot is placed on the ball, the weight of the body is transferred on to it, so that when the dancer travels while so placing the foot, a step is taken.

(d) *Heel.* When the heel is in contact with the ground, with the sole of the foot kept straight and inclined upwards, the working foot is said to be placed on the *heel*.

2

The heel is always placed without pressure, except in the Eighth Seann Triubhas Step, in which the weight is momentarily taken on it.

When the working foot is placed on the heel in any open position except Fourth-opposite-Fifth, the knee of the working leg is kept straight.

Certain positions have *rear* and/or *aerial* equivalents. There is no rear or aerial equivalent to First Position or to Third Crossed Position. There is an aerial equivalent, but no rear equivalent to Second Position. Conversely there is a rear equivalent but no aerial equivalent to Fourth-opposite-Fifth Position and to the Fifth Position. Every other position has a rear and an aerial equivalent.

In a *Rear Position*, the working foot is never placed on the half point or the heel.

In an *open aerial position*, the knee of the working leg should be kept straight, and the working foot, with the instep well arched, is off the ground with the toe at the correct height in relation to the supporting leg, to give *normal* level (in line with the centre of the calf), *high* level (in line with the centre of the knee-cap), or *low* level (in line with the ankle).

In the two *closed aerial positions*, namely Third Aerial Position and Third Rear Aerial Position, the working foot is off the ground in contact with, and at the correct height in relation to the supporting leg to give *normal* level (foot vertical—heel in line with the hollow below the knee) or, in the case of Third Aerial Position only, *low* level (foot vertical—toe at ankle height) or *very low* level (see note to the description of Shuffle on page 31).

Note.—In all Aerial Positions (Open or Closed), normal level is to be understood where no particular height is specified.

When preparing for and/or landing from a step of elevation with the weight equally distributed on the balls of both feet in Third or Fifth Position, the insteps should be as fully arched as possible, the heels equidistant from the ground, and the knees slightly relaxed.

The Line of Direction

The Line of Direction is an imaginary line on the ground, passing from front to back between the heels of the dancer when standing in First Position. The angles of basic foot positions are measured from this line.

First Position

The heels are together, with the weight of the body equally distributed on both feet, which are turned out to form an angle of 90° (each foot being at an angle of 45° from the Line of Direction). The dancer may be standing with both feet flat on the ground (1), or may be poised on the balls of the feet (2).

Second
Aerial Position

The working leg is extended to the side as in Second Position, but raised at the required level—low (5), normal (6), or high (7).

4

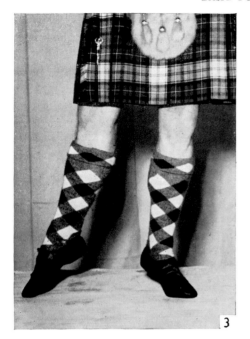

Second Position

The working leg is extended directly to the side at an angle of 90° from the Line of Direction, the toe and heel of the working foot being in line with the heel of the supporting foot (4). The working foot may be placed on the toe (3), half point, ball, or heel and, except in the latter case, is placed approximately one and a half foot-lengths from the heel of the supporting foot.

Third Position

The working foot, which may be placed on the toe (9), half point, ball (8), or heel, touches the hollow of the supporting foot, each foot facing outwards at an angle of 90° from the other (or 45° from the Line of Direction).

Note

When the weight is equally distributed on the balls of both feet, the sole of the front foot is directly over the instep of the rear foot.

6

Third Aerial Position

The outside edge of the working foot is in contact with the front of the supporting leg, with the sole vertical so that no part of the foot projects beyond either side of the supporting leg. The knee of the working leg is pressed well back and the working foot is raised to the correct height to give *normal* level (heel placed just below the knee-cap of the supporting leg (10), or *low* level (toe in line with the ankle of supporting leg).

Note.—For the description of a variation of the above position called 'Third Aerial Position Very Low' see note to Shuffle on page 31.

Third Rear Position

The hollow of the working foot touches the heel of the supporting foot, each foot facing outwards at an angle of 90° from the other (11, 12). The working foot may be placed on the toe or ball.

13

14

Third Rear Aerial Position

The working foot is placed vertically behind the supporting leg at the same height as in Third Aerial Position normal level, the inside edge of the foot being in contact with the calf of the supporting leg (14). The knee of the working leg is held well back, no part of the working foot being visible from the front (13).

15

Third Crossed Position

The working leg is crossed in front of the supporting leg with the half point of the working foot placed near the outside edge of the instep of the supporting foot (15).

Fourth Position

The working leg is extended to the front. The working foot, which is placed only on the toe, is turned out at an angle of 45° from the Line of Direction, with the heel directly in line with the heel of the supporting foot (16).

Fourth Aerial Position

The working leg is extended to the front as in Fourth Position, but raised at the required level (17).

9

Fourth Rear Position. As in Fourth Position, but the working leg is extended to the rear, and is placed only on the ball (18).

Fourth Rear Aerial Position. The working leg is extended to the rear as in Fourth Rear Position, but raised at the required level (19).

Fourth Intermediate Position. The working leg is extended diagonally forward at an angle of 45° from the Line of Direction (between Second and Fourth Position) with the working foot placed on the toe (20), half point or ball.

Fourth Intermediate Aerial Position. The working leg is extended as in Fourth Intermediate Position, but raised at the required level (21).

Fourth Intermediate Rear Position. As in Fourth Intermediate Position, but the working leg is extended to the rear and is placed only on the ball (22).

Fourth Intermediate Rear Aerial Position. As in Fourth Intermediate Rear Position, but with the working leg raised at the required level (23).

20

21

22

23

Fourth-opposite-Fifth Position

The working leg is extended to the front as in Fourth Position, but with the toe of the working foot in line with the heel of the supporting foot and with a slight relaxation of the knee of the working leg. The working foot may be placed on the toe (24), half point or heel and, in the latter case, the heel is placed in line with the toe of the supporting foot.

Note.—This position is used only in the Sword Dance.

Fourth-opposite-Fifth Rear Position

This is the position of the rear foot when the front foot is placed in Fourth-opposite-Fifth Position.

24

Fifth Position

The working foot is in contact with the big toe joint of the supporting foot, and may be placed on the toe (25), half point, ball, or heel, each foot facing outwards at an angle of 90° from the other.

Note.—When the weight of the body is equally distributed on the balls of both feet, the sole of the front foot is directly over the toes of the rear foot.

Fifth Rear Position

This is the position of the rear foot when it is placed on the ball with the big toe joint in contact with the front foot, each foot facing outwards at an angle of 90° from the other.

25

2 ARM POSITIONS

First Position

Both hands rest on the hips with the backs of the hands
to the front, the knuckles facing the body with the wrists
straight, and the elbows pointing directly out to the
side (26).

Note.—When an arm is raised or lowered, there should be a minimum displace-
ment of the elbow, and no part of the arm or hand should come in front of
the dancer's face. An exception is in the First and Second Steps of the Seann
Triubhas where the arms are circled and the hands come up in front of the face.

Second Position. One arm is placed as in First Position, the other is raised at the side, with the arm and wrist slightly curved, the hand slightly above and forward from the head-line, the palm turned towards the face (27, 28).

Note.—In this position the raised arm is always on the side opposite to the working leg, except in a Propelled Pivot Turn.

Third Position. Both arms are placed as described for the raised arm in Second Position (29).

Fourth Position. A closer and higher form of Third Position with the hands almost touching (30).

Fifth Position. The arms are curved in front of the body, with the fingers grouped, and the hands almost touching. The palms are facing the body at arms length, and slightly below waist-line (31, 32).

Note.—Grouping of fingers : the fingers are lightly grouped and the thumb is in contact with the first joint of the middle finger.

29

30

31

32

3 HEAD POSITIONS

All head positions are described in relation to the position of the body.

First Position

The head faces the front with the eyes level (33).

Note.—The head is in First Position when the *arms* are in First, Third, Fourth or Fifth Position, except when otherwise stated (33).

33

Second Position

The head is directed diagonally to the right (34) or left (35), with the chin slightly raised.

Note.—When the *arms* are in Second Position the head is turned away from the raised arm.

34

35

§ B

BASIC MOVEMENTS

The system on which the counting of movements is based is explained in Chapter 3.

The Bow

Stand with the *feet* and *head* in First Position, *arms* by the side or in First Position. Bow by inclining the body forward slowly, and return to the original position (36, 37, 38).

Note.—The depth of the bow must not be exaggerated, and the timing varies according to each dance, as described in Chapter 2.

36

37

38

39

Hop

A movement of elevation begun on the ball of one foot and finished by landing on the ball of the same foot.

Spring

As for Hop, but landing on the ball of the other foot (39, 40, 41).

Assemble

A movement of elevation begun on the ball of one foot and finished by landing simultaneously on the balls of both feet in Third or Fifth Position (42, 43, 44).

Disassemble

A movement of elevation begun in a closed position with the weight of the body equally distributed on the balls of both feet, and finished by landing on the ball of one foot with the other placed in, or raised to, a specified position.

Note.—There is no travel on this movement, and, unless otherwise stated, during the elevation there is no extension of the foot upon which the dancer is to land.

42

Change

A movement of elevation begun with the weight of the body on the balls of both feet in Fifth Position and finished by landing on the balls of both feet simultaneously in Fifth Position with the other foot in front (45, 46, 47).

Note.—During the elevation there is no extension towards Second Aerial Position. This movement may also be executed using Third Position.

Brush

(a) Outwards : The working foot lightly touches the ground in its progress from Third Aerial Position Low to an Open Aerial Position or from a Rear Open Aerial Position Low, through First Position, to Fourth Aerial Position. (b) Inwards : The working foot lightly touches the ground in its progress from an Open Aerial Position to Third Aerial Position Low.

Note.—When an outward Brush is executed in conjunction with a Spring or a Hop, the working foot touches the floor almost simultaneously on landing.

Leap

A movement of elevation begun from the balls of both feet in Fifth Position, extending both legs towards Second Aerial Position, and finished by landing simultaneously on the balls of both feet in Fifth Position with or without change of feet (48, 49, 50).

Note 1.—On the extension during the elevation, both legs should be straightened.

Note 2.—This movement may also be executed using Third Position.

Shake

The working foot is progressively extended by two or more subsidiary movements from an accepted closed

45

position to an accepted open aerial position. The Shakes so produced come from the knee, controlled by the thigh.

48

46

47

49

50

Pas de Basque

Preparing with an extension of the working foot to Second Aerial Position Low (51, 52) ; spring to that side (53), bringing the new working foot to Third or Fifth Position, placing it on the half point (54) ; then beat (without exaggeration) the ball of the other foot in Third or Fifth Rear Position, at the same time sharply extending the front foot, if required, to begin the next movement.

Note 1.—The same Position—Third or Fifth—must be used throughout the movement.

Note 2.—When a turn, or part of a turn, is executed using two Pas de Basque, there is no extension to finish the first Pas de Basque, and the second is danced with little or no travel.

Note 3.—This movement may also be danced with other than lateral travel, in which case the extension of the starting foot is along the required line of travel, generally towards Fourth Intermediate Position.

53

54

Counting

(2 Pas de Basque)

Reel	1 & 2	3 & 4	= (2 bars)
Sword Dance	1& 2	3& 4	= (1 bar)

Open Pas de Basque

As in Pas de Basque, except that the front foot is placed in Fourth-opposite-Fifth Position, and there is no sharp extension at the finish.

Note.—This movement is used only in the Sword Dance, and in the quick steps is also executed using Fourth Intermediate Position and Second Position.

55

56

High Cut

Spring, hop or disassemble and, simultaneously on landing, take the working foot to Third Rear Aerial Position (55), having first extended that foot towards Second Aerial Position during the elevation ; then (working from the knee joint only) quickly re-extend the working foot towards Second Aerial Position (56) and return it sharply to Third Rear Aerial Position (57). There is no side travel in this movement.

Note.—Performed in series, High Cutting can be described as a succession of Springs from Third Rear Aerial Position to Third Rear Aerial Position, executing a High Cut each time and during each elevation extending both feet towards Second Aerial Position, although this extension of the foot from which each Spring is commenced may be slight.

Counting

(four High Cuts)

(*a*) To Strathspey tempo—$_1$& $_2$& $_3$& $_4$&
In certain stated instances a single High Cut may be counted
1 and (and)

(*b*) To Reel tempo—1 & 2 & 3 & 4 &
In certain stated instances, a single High Cut may be counted
$_1$& or 1 and (and)

High Cut in Front

As for High Cut, but the raised foot is taken to Third Aerial Position (58).

Note.—High Cuts in Front are not performed in series, and if this movement is preceded or followed by an extension of the working foot to Fourth Intermediate Aerial Position or Fourth Intermediate Position, then the extension executed by the working foot during the Cut is made towards Fourth Intermediate Aerial Position instead of Second Aerial Position.

59 60

Balance

Starting with one foot in Fourth Intermediate Aerial Position, spring on to that foot displacing the supporting foot which is taken to Fourth Intermediate Rear Aerial Position. Repeat *contra* to complete the movement and finish in the starting position. This movement occupies two beats of music.

Travelling Balance

Begun with the right foot in Fourth Intermediate Aerial Position, the *arms* in Third Position, the right shoulder slightly advanced with the head in Second Position turned to the right (59). Bring the right foot inwards and place it on the ball to displace the left foot (60), with which a step is taken to Fourth Intermediate Rear Position (61); place the ball of the right foot in Third or Fifth Position (62), extending the left foot to Fourth Intermediate Rear Aerial Position (63). During this part of the movement, which travels in a straight line in a diagonal direction approximately 45° to the Line of Direction, the *arms* are taken to Fourth Position (count '1 & 2'). The above is now repeated *contra*, travelling forward along the same diagonal line, taking the *arms* back to Third Position to finish the movement in the original starting position (count '3 & 4'). This movement can also be executed on the other side with the opposite foot.

Note.—The upper part of the body should be held steady.

26

61

62

Rock

Spring from Third or Fifth Position to Third Rear Position, or vice versa, pointing the working foot almost simultaneously on landing. Rocks are usually danced in series, in which case the first Rock may be executed starting from an open position. The rear foot is always pointed first.

Note.—When the working foot is pointed during this movement the toe touches the ground lightly.

63

Shedding or Round-the-Leg

Hop, taking the working foot to Third Rear Aerial Position (64); hop, passing the working foot to Third Aerial Position (65); hop, passing the working foot back to Third Rear Aerial Position (66).

Note.—The working foot must be perpendicular during the passing and kept as close to the supporting leg as possible. The knee of the working leg must be held well back : all movement of the working leg is from the knee downwards. This movement is always begun from an open position.

64

Toe-and-Heel

Hop or spring and, almost simultaneously on landing, point the working foot in a specified position, then hop and, almost simultaneously on landing, place the heel of the working foot in the same specified position. This movement occupies two beats of music.

Note 1.—The toe and the heel must touch the ground lightly and the working foot must be kept fairly low.

Note 2.—The specified position for this movement may be Second, Third, Fourth-opposite-Fifth, or Fifth.

Heel-and-Toe

Hop, placing the heel of the working foot in Second Position ; hop, pointing the working foot in Third or Fifth Position. This movement occupies two beats of music.

Back-stepping

Starting with one foot in Third Aerial Position, pass that foot quickly (as in Shedding) to Third Rear Aerial Position, and, with a Spring, slide it down the back of the supporting leg, bringing the other foot quickly to Third Aerial Position. Repeat as required. This movement may also be executed starting or finishing in Third Rear Aerial Position. Each Back-step occupies one beat of music.

Shuffle

Begin with one foot in Fourth Intermediate Aerial Position Low, spring, and during the elevation extend the supporting foot to Fourth Intermediate Aerial Position Low, then, almost simultaneously on landing, brush the new working foot inwards to Third Aerial Position Very Low and immediately brush it outwards to Fourth Intermediate Aerial Position Low.

Note 1.—In the above Third Aerial Position Very Low, the instep of the working foot is slightly relaxed, the toe slightly off the ground, and the heel over the instep of the supporting foot. This position is frequently referred to as ' over the buckle'.

Note 2.—Unless otherwise stated, this movement is executed without any lateral or forward travel.

Counting

(four Shuffles)

(a) To Strathspey tempo $_1$& $_2$& $_3$& $_4$&

(b) To Reel tempo   1 & 2 & 3 & 4 &

29

67   68

Spring Point

Spring, and point the working foot in an open position, both feet touching the ground almost simultaneously (67, 68).

Pivot Turn

(*a*) *Turning to the left.* Take the right foot to Third Crossed Position while beginning to pivot to the left on the ball of the left foot (69), and complete the turn on the balls of both feet without displacing them (70), finishing in Third or Fifth Position with the left foot in front.

(*b*) *Turning to the right.* As above, but starting with the left foot and finishing with the right foot in front.

Note.—The working foot may be extended to Fourth Intermediate Aerial Position before starting the Pivot Turn.

Propelled Pivot Turn or Reel Turn

Danced during a Reel by two dancers, facing in opposite directions with the shoulder-lines parallel. The *inner arm* of each dancer is extended diagonally forward and linked with that of the partner, the *outer arm* being in Second Position, and the head turned slightly towards partner.

69

70

71

Note.—' The inner arms linked '— The inner forearms rest parallel and are in contact with each other, with the palm of the hand lightly supporting the underside of partner's arm just above the elbow. Since this is not a grip but an aid to balance, the thumb must not encircle partner's upper arm (71).

When danced turning to the right, the movement is begun by the partners moving forward on the right foot whilst linking their right arms and adopting the position described above (count ' 1 ') ; they now place the left foot on the half point in Second Position, to allow for a slight travel of the right foot (count ' & 2 ') ; the turn is now continued by repeating the actions described for the count of ' & 2 ' as often as required (count ' & 3 & 4 ', etc.) so that, while the right foot takes the main weight of the body, the left foot acts as a propelling force to produce the turn, during which the knees must be slightly relaxed.

When danced turning to the left, the movement is begun by moving forward on to the left foot whilst linking left arms ; the left foot then becomes the main supporting foot with the right foot providing the propelling force.

31

Progressive Strathspey Movement

Beginning with the right foot in Third Aerial Position, step with that foot along the line of travel to Fourth Intermediate Position (count ' 1 ') ; close the ball of the left foot to Third or Fifth Rear Position, extending the right foot to Fourth Intermediate Aerial Position (count ' 2 ') ; spring on the right foot along the line of travel bringing the left foot to Third Rear Aerial Position (count ' 3 ') ; hop on the right foot with slight forward travel, passing the left foot as in Shedding to Third Aerial Position (count ' 4 ').

Note.—On the first two counts the body is at an angle of 45° to the line of travel with the right shoulder leading ; on the third count, the body faces the line of travel ; on the fourth count, the body is at an angle of 45° to the line of travel with the left shoulder leading.

The movement may be executed with the opposite foot.

The head is always directed along the line of travel.

Progressive Reel Movement

Hop on the left foot taking the right foot to Third Aerial Position Low, then step with the right foot along the line of travel to Fourth Intermediate Position (count ' & 1 ') ; close the ball of the left foot to Third or Fifth Rear Position then, with slight elevation, spring on the right foot along the line of travel (count ' & 2 ').

The movement may be executed with the opposite foot.

Note.—The body is used as for the Progressive Strathspey Movement, beginning to change the shoulder lead on the forward step which follows each hop.

§C. BASIC STEPS

A Basic Step is a combination of Basic Movements.

A detailed description of the Steps which may be used in Championship Highland Dances is given in Chapter 2.

Chapter Two

HIGHLAND DANCES

A Dance is a combination of a number of Basic Steps. In the following descriptions of the Dances the following abbreviations are used :

RF = Right foot.   LF = Left foot.

All dances should be preceded by an introduction of four bars of music.

With reference to foot work only, where Fifth Position is used in describing a step in any dance, Third Position may be substituted but, throughout that step, the same position—Third or Fifth—should be used.

In each of the following dances, the first and last steps given should always be performed as such, an exception being the Seann Triubhas, in which any of the quick steps may be used as a last step. The other steps may be performed in a different numerical order to that given in this book.

As a signal for the piper to change from slow to quick tempo the dancer may clap hands on the last beat of the slow step.

1 THE HIGHLAND FLING

A Solo Dance consisting normally of six or eight steps danced without travel.

MUSIC : ' Monymusk ' or any other suitable Strathspey tune.

Tempo : $\downarrow$ = 152 (or 38 bars to the minute).

The arms, when changing from one position to another, do so between the last beat of one bar and the first beat of the next bar, except where specially mentioned in the Sixth (Cross-over) Step.

Note.—In the following description, the beginning of each step is given on the assumption that the steps are being performed in the numerical order given, but, should the order be varied, the movement with which each step begins (Hop or Spring) is determined by the finishing position of the preceding step.

INTRODUCTION

Bars 1 and 2—Stand as for Bow.

Bars 3 and 4—Bow (count ' 1, 2, 3, 4, 5, 6 ') ; rise on balls of feet, taking *arms* to First Position on the seventh count, if not already so placed (count ' 7, 8 ').

FIRST STEP—FIRST SHEDDING or ROUND-THE-LEG

Bar 1—Disassemble, pointing RF in Second Position (count ' 1 ') ; execute Round-the-Leg movement with RF (count ' 2, 3, 4 ').

33

Bar 2—Beginning with Spring RF (instead of Disassemble), repeat Bar 1 with the other foot (count 5, 6, 7, 8 ').

Bar 3—Beginning with Spring LF (instead of Disassemble), repeat Bar 1 (count ' 1, 2, 3, 4 ').

Bar 4—Spring RF, pointing LF in Second Position (count ' 5 ') ; make a complete turn to the right, with approximately one-third of a turn on each count, executing Round-the-Leg movement with LF (count ' 6, 7, 8 ').

Arms

Second Position in Bars 1, 2 and 3 ; First or Second Position in Bar 4.

Bars 5 to 8—Beginning with Hop RF (instead of Disassemble), repeat Bars 1 to 4 with the opposite foot, turning to the left on Bar 8.

SECOND STEP—FIRST BACK-STEPPING

Bar 1—Hop LF, pointing RF in Second Position (count ' 1 ') ; hop LF, taking RF to Third Rear Aerial Position (count ' 2 ') ; hop LF, pointing RF in Second Position (count ' 3 ') ; hop LF, taking RF to Third Aerial Position (count ' 4 ').

Bar 2—Execute back-stepping, springing RF, LF, RF, LF (count ' 5, 6, 7, 8 ').

Arms

Second Position in Bar 1 ; Third Position in Bar 2.

Bars 3 and 4—Beginning with Spring (instead of Hop), repeat Bars 1 and 2 with the opposite foot.

Bars 5 to 8—Beginning with Spring (instead of Hop), repeat Bars 1 to 4.

THIRD STEP—TOE-AND-HEEL

Bar 1—Spring LF, pointing RF in Second Position, then execute Shedding as in Bar 1 of the First Step (count ' 1, 2, 3, 4 ').

Bar 2—Spring, then hop on RF, executing Toe-and-Heel movement with LF in Fifth Position (count ' 5, 6 ') ; spring, then hop on LF, executing Toe-and-Heel movement with RF in Fifth Position (count ' 7, 8 ').

Bar 3—Repeat Bar 2 (count ' 1, 2, 3, 4 ').

Bar 4—Turn to the right as in Bar 4 of the First Step (count ' 5, 6, 7, 8 ').

Arms

Second Position in Bar 1 ; First Position in Bars 2 and 3 ; First or Second Position in Bar 4.

Bars 5 to 8—Beginning with Hop (instead of Spring) repeat Bars 1 to 4 with the opposite foot, turning to the left on Bar 8.

FOURTH STEP—ROCKING

Bar 1—Hop LF, pointing RF in Second Position (count ' 1 ') ; hop LF, taking RF to Third Rear Aerial Position (count ' 2 ') ; hop LF, pointing RF in Fifth Position (count ' 3 ') ; hop LF, extending RF with Shake to Fourth Intermediate Aerial Position (count ' 4 ').

Bar 2—Execute four Rocks, beginning with Spring RF (count ' 5, 6, 7, 8 ').

Arms

Second Position in Bar 1 ; Third Position in Bar 2.

Bars 3 and 4—Beginning with Spring (instead of Hop), repeat Bars 1 and 2 with the opposite foot.

Bars 5 to 8—Beginning with Spring (instead of Hop), repeat Bars 1 to 4.

FIFTH STEP—SECOND BACK-STEPPING

Bar 1—Spring LF, pointing RF in Second Position (count ' 1 ') ; hop LF, taking RF to Third Rear Aerial Position (count ' 2 '), pass RF quickly (as in Shedding) to Third Aerial Position, then hop LF, extending RF to Fourth Intermediate Aerial Position (count ' &3 ') ; hop LF, returning RF to Third Aerial Position (count ' 4 ').

Bar 2—Execute back-stepping, springing RF, LF, RF, LF (count ' 5, 6, 7, 8 ').

Arms

Second Position in Bar 1 ; Third Position in Bar 2.

Bars 3 and 4—Repeat Bars 1 and 2 with the opposite foot.

Bars 5 to 8—Repeat Bars 1 to 4.

ALTERNATIVE METHOD

Bar 1—Spring LF, extending RF to Fourth Intermediate Aerial Position (count ' 1 ') ; hop LF, executing a High Cut in front with RF (count ' 2& ') ;

hop LF, extending RF to Fourth Intermediate Aerial Position (count ' 3 ') ; hop LF, returning RF to Third Aerial Position (count ' 4 ').

Bar 2—Execute back-stepping, springing RF, LF, RF, LF (count ' 5, 6, 7, 8 ').

Arms

Second Position in Bar 1 ; Third Position in Bar 2.

Bars 3 and 4—Repeat Bars 1 and 2 with the opposite foot.

Bars 5 to 8—Repeat Bars 1 to 4.

SIXTH STEP—CROSS-OVER

Bar 1—Execute Bar 1 of the Third Step—Shedding with RF (count ' 1, 2, 3, 4 ').

Bar 2—Hop LF, pointing RF in Second Position (count ' 5 ') ; hop LF, taking RF to Third Rear Aerial Position (count ' 6 ') ; passing RF through Third Aerial Position, and down in front of the supporting leg, spring on to it raising LF to Third Rear Aerial Position—or extending LF to Second Aerial Position Low—(count ' 7 ') ; hop RF pointing LF in Fifth Position (count ' 8 ').

Arms

Second Position, changing to Second Position on the other side on the seventh count.

Bars 3 and 4—Beginning with Hop (instead of Spring), repeat Bars 1 and 2 with the opposite foot.

Bars 5 to 8—Beginning with Hop (instead of Spring), repeat Bars 1 to 4.

SEVENTH STEP—SHAKE AND TURN

Bar 1—Execute Bar 1 of the Fourth Step (Point and Shake) (count ' 1, 2, 3, 4 ').

Bar 2—Turn to right as in Bar 4 of the First Step (count ' 5, 6, 7, 8 ').

Arms

Second Position in Bar 1 ; First or Second Position in Bar 2.

Bars 3 and 4—Repeat Bars 1 and 2 with the opposite foot.

Bars 5 to 8—Repeat Bars 1 to 4.

ALTERNATIVE SEVENTH STEP—DOUBLE SHAKE AND ROCK

Bar 1—Beginning with Hop LF (instead of Disassemble), execute Shedding with RF, as in Bar 1 of the First Step (count ' 1, 2, 3, 4 ').

Bar 2—Hop LF, pointing RF in Fifth Position (count ' 5 ') ; hop LF, extending RF with shake to Fourth Intermediate Aerial Position (count ' 6 ') ; repeat counts ' 5, 6 ' (count ' 7, 8 ').

Bar 3—Execute four Rocks as in Bar 2 of the Fourth Step (count ' 1, 2, 3, 4 ').

Bar 4—Turn to the right as in Bar 4 of the First Step (count ' 5, 6, 7, 8 ').

Arms

Second Position in Bars 1 and 2 ; Third Position in Bar 3 ; First or Second Position in Bar 4.

Bars 5 to 8—Repeat Bars 1 to 4 with the opposite foot, turning to the left in Bar 8.

EIGHTH STEP—LAST SHEDDING or ROUND-THE-LEG

Bar 1—Beginning with Hop LF (instead of Dissassemble) execute Shedding with RF as in Bar 1 of the First Step (count ' 1, 2, 3, 4 ').

Bars 2 and 3—Repeat Bar 1 twice (count ' 5, 6, 7, 8, 1, 2, 3, 4 ').

Bar 4—Turn to the right as in Bar 4 of the First Step (count ' 5, 6, 7, 8 ').

Arms

Second Position in Bars 1, 2 and 3 : First or Second Position in Bar 4.

Bar 5—Execute Bar 5 of the First Step—Shedding with LF (count ' 1, 2, 3, 4 ').

Bar 6—Repeat Bar 5 (count ' 5, 6, 7, 8 ').

Bar 7—Turn to the left as in Bar 8 of the First Step (count ' 1, 2, 3, 4 ').

Bar 8—Repeat Bar 7 (count ' 5, 6, 7, 8 ').

Arms

Second Position in Bars 5 and 6 ; First or Second Position in Bars 7 and 8.

FIRST ALTERNATIVE, LAST SHEDDING A

Bars 1 to 6—As for above (Shedding three times with RF, then turn ; Shedding twice with LF).

Bar 7—Repeat Bar 6 (Shedding with LF).

Bar 8—Turn to the left as in Bar 8 of the First Step.

SECOND ALTERNATIVE, LAST SHEDDING B

Bars 1 to 6—As for above.

Bar 7—Spring LF and turn to left as in Bar 8 of the First Step.

Bar 8—Spring RF and turn to right as in Bar 4 of the First Step.

FINISH

Step to the right with RF and close LF to RF in First Position (flat) and bow.

2 THE SWORD DANCE (GILLIE CHALUIM)

A Solo Dance consisting usually of not more than five or six steps of which the first four are danced to a slow tempo.

Music : ' Gillie Chaluim '

Tempo 1 (Slow) : ♩ = 128 (or 32 bars to the minute).

Tempo 2 (Quick) : ♩ = 184 (or 46 bars to the minute).

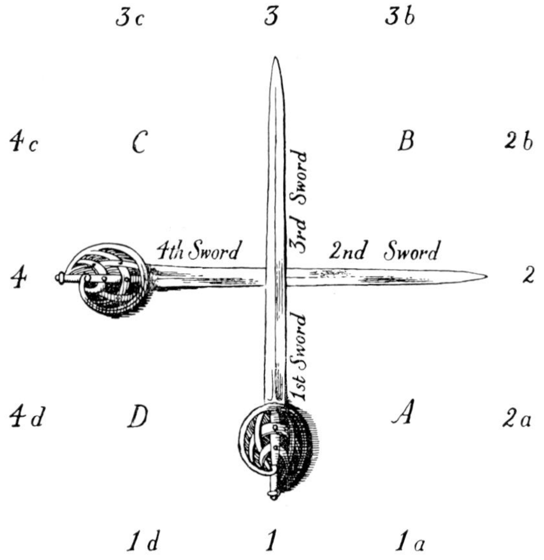

This dance is performed round and over two Highland broadswords placed crosswise on the ground at right angles to each other. The top sword is in a direct line from front to back, with the hilt (called the top hilt) towards the dancer and with the centre of its blade directly above the centre of the blade of the other sword, the hilt of which is to the dancer's left. The hilts are placed as shown in the diagram.

38

Although only two swords are used it has been found expedient to refer to the half blade nearest the dancer's starting place (near the top hilt) as the First Sword then, working in an anti-clockwise direction, referring to the other half blades as the Second, Third and Fourth Swords.

The areas within the four right angles formed by the crossed swords are termed 'spaces', the space between the First and Second Swords being denoted by the letter *A* and the other spaces, taking an anti-clockwise direction, by the letters *B*, *C* and *D*.

In the diagram the spot on the ground, approximately one foot-length from the top hilt and directly in line with the First Sword, is marked by the number 1, the spots on the ground about one and a half foot-lengths directly to the right and left of the above spot being marked by the auxiliary numbers and letters 1a and 1d respectively. Similarly, the corresponding spots on the ground in relation to the two sword points and the other hilt are marked by the appropriate numbers and auxiliary letters.

While dancing over or across the swords the head may be slightly inclined to allow the dancer to see the swords.

Note 1.—Where Open Pas de Basque and Spring Point are mentioned in the description of the following steps, the supporting foot is given first.

Note 2.—The amount of turn at the end of each step is determined by the starting position of the step which follows.

Note 3.—When executing a Pas de Basque 'inside' the swords, there is no sharp extension at the end.

TEMPO 1

INTRODUCTION

Bars 1 and 2—Stand at 1 as for the Bow.

Bars 3 and 4—Bow (count ' 1, 2, 3, 4, 5, 6 ') ; bring *arms* to First Position, if not already so placed (count ' 7, 8 ').

FIRST STEP—ADDRESSING THE SWORDS

Bar 1—Pas de Basque to 1a with RF (count ' $_1$& 2 ') ; Pas de Basque to 1d with LF (count ' $_3$& 4 ').

Bar 2—Execute a three-quarter turn to the right with two Pas de Basque (making approximately three-eights turn on each), the first Pas de Basque with RF to 1a (count ' $_5$& 6 ') ; the second Pas de Basque with LF finishing at 2a (count ' $_7$& 8 ').

Bar 3—Pas de Basque to 2B with RF (count ' $_1$& 2 ') ; assemble at 2 with RF in front (count ' 3 ') ; disassemble, taking RF to Third Rear Aerial Position, having extended that foot towards Second Aerial Position

39

during the elevation—the LF may also be extended to Second Aerial Position during the elevation—(count ' 4 ').

Bar 4—Execute four High Cuts at 2, springing RF, LF, RF, LF (count '₁& ₂& ₃& ₄& ').

Arms

First Position in Bars 1, 2 and 3, changing to Third Position on the fourth count of Bar 3; Third Position on Bar 4.

Bars 5 to 8—As for Bars 1 to 4, starting at 2 and finishing at 3.

Bars 9 to 12—As above, starting at 3 and finishing at 4.

Bars 13 to 16—As above, starting at 4 and finishing at 1.

SECOND STEP—OPEN PAS DE BASQUE

Bar 1—Pas de Basque into *A* with RF (count '₁& 2 '); Pas de Basque into *D* with LF (count '₃& 4 ').

Bar 2—Open Pas de Basque into *A* with RF, LF Fourth-opposite-Fifth Position in *B* (count '₅& 6 '); Open Pas de Basque into *D* with LF, RF Fourth-opposite-Fifth Position in *C* (count '₇& 8 ').

Bar 3—Repeat Bar 2 (count '₁& 2, ₃& 4 ').

Bar 4—Execute four Spring Points turning over the Second Sword—RF in *A*, LF Fourth Position in B (count ' 5 '); with half turn to right, LF in B, RF Fourth Position in *A* (count '6 '); RF in B, LF Fourth Position in *A* (count '7'); with quarter turn to right, LF in *A*, RF Second Position in *B* (count ' 8 ').

Arms

First Position in Bar 1; Third Position in Bars 2 and 3; First Position in Bar 4.

Bars 5 to 8—As for Bars 1 to 4, finishing with the Spring Points turning over the Third Sword.

Bars 9 to 12—As for Bars 1 to 4, finishing with the Spring Points turning over the Fourth Sword.

Bars 13 to 16—As for Bars 1 to 4, finishing with the Spring Points turning over the First Sword.

Note.—If the third (Toe-and-Heel) Step or the Seventh (Quick) or Eighth (Quick) Step with the Alternative Method for the First Bar is to follow, then, on the last Spring Point in Bar 16, make half a turn to the right finishing LF in *D*, RF Fourth Position in *A*.

THIRD STEP—TOE-AND-HEEL

Begun with the dancer facing *A* with LF (supporting foot) in *D*, RF pointed in Fifth Position or pointed in Fourth Position in *A*.

Bar 1—Spring, then three Hops RF in *D*, while executing the Toe-and-Heel movement twice with the working foot (LF) Fourth-opposite-Fifth Position in *A* (count ' 1, 2, 3, 4 ').

Bar 2—Repeat Bar 1 reversing the positions of the feet (count ' 5, 6, 7, 8 ').

Bar 3—With quarter turn to left on the first count, spring into *A* with RF, then hop RF in *A*, executing one Toe-and-Heel movement with LF in Fifth Position (count ' 1, 2 ') ; spring, then hop LF in *A*, executing one Toe-and-Heel movement with RF in Fifth Position (count ' 3, 4 ').

Bar 4—Execute four Spring Points over the Second Sword, each with the supporting foot in *A* and the working foot Fourth Position in *B* (count ' 5, 6, 7, 8 ').

Arms

Second Position (R arm up) in Bar 1 ; Second Position (L arm up) in Bar 2 ; First Position in Bar 3 ; Third Position in Bar 4.

Bars 5 to 8—As for Bars 1 to 4, finishing over the Third Sword.

Bars 9 to 12—As for Bars 1 to 4, finishing over the Fourth Sword.

Bars 13 and 14—As for Bars 1 and 2 (over the Fourth Sword).

Bar 15 *—With half turn to right, Pas de Basque with RF into *D*, travelling towards 1 (count ' $_1$& 2 ') ; assemble at 1 with RF in front (count ' 3 ') ; disassemble as in Bar 3 of the First Step (count ' 4 ').

Bar 16—Execute four High Cuts at 1 as in the First Step, with *arms* in Third Position (count ' $_5$& $_6$& $_7$& $_8$& ').

Note.—If the alternative method is used the Note to the Second Step applies also to this Step, with reference to the Seventh and Eighth Steps.

FOURTH STEP—POINTING

Bar 1—Pas de Basque into *A* with RF (count ' $_1$& 2 ') ; Pas de Basque into *D* with LF (count ' $_3$& 4 ').

* Alternatively :

Bar 15—As for Bar 3, but in *D*.

Bar 16—Execute four Spring Points over the First Sword, turning as described in Bar 4 of the Second Step.

Bar 2—Spring Point with RF in *A*, LF Second Position in *D* (count ' 5 ') ; hop RF, pointing LF in Fifth Position (count ' 6 ') ; hop RF, pointing LF Fourth Position in *B* (count ' 7 '); hop RF, bringing LF back to point it in Fifth Position (count ' 8 ').

Bar 3—Spring Point with LF in *D*, RF Second Position in *A* (count ' 1 ') ; hop LF, pointing RF in Fifth Position (count ' 2 ') ; hop LF, pointing RF Fourth Position in *C* (count ' 3 '); hop LF, bringing RF back to point it in Fifth Position (count ' 4 ').

Bar 4—Spring Point with RF in *A*, LF Second Position in *D* (count ' 5 ') ; with quarter turn to left, hop RF pointing LF in Fifth Position (count ' 6 ') ; Spring Point with LF in *A*, RF Second Position in *B* (count ' 7 ') ; hop LF, bringing RF back to point it in Fifth Position (count ' 8 ').

Arms

First Position in Bar 1 ; Second Position (R arm up) in Bar 2 ; Second Position (L arm up) in Bar 3 ; First Position in Bar 4.

Bars 5 to 8—As for Bars 1 to 4 finishing in *B*.

Bars 9 to 12—As for Bars 1 to 4 finishing in *C*.

Bars 13 to 16—As for Bars 1 to 4 finishing in *D*.

Note.—If this Step is to be followed by the Third Step or by the Seventh or Eighth Step with the Alternative Method for the First Bar, then Bar 16 should be executed as follows : Spring Point into *D* with RF, LF Second Position in *C* ('count 5 ') ; hop RF, pointing LF in Fifth Position (count ' 6 ') ; Spring Point with LF in *D*, RF Fourth Position in *A* (count ' 7 ') ; hop LF, bringing RF back to point it in Fifth Position (count ' 8 ').

FIFTH STEP—DIAGONAL POINTS

Bar 1—Pas de Basque into *A* with RF, then into *D* with LF as in Bar 1 of the Fourth Step (count ' ₁& 2, ₃& 4 ').

Bar 2—Open Pas de Basque into *A* with RF, LF Fourth-opposite-Fifth Position in *B* (count ' ₅& 6 ') ; Spring Point with LF in *D*, RF Fourth Intermediate Position in *B* (count ' 7 ') ; Spring Point with RF in *A*, LF Fourth Intermediate Position in *C* (count ' 8 ').

Bar 3—Open Pas de Basque into D with LF, RF Fourth-opposite-Fifth Position in *C* (count ' ₁& 2 ') ; Spring Point with RF in *A*, LF Fourth Intermediate Position in *C* (count ' 3 ') ; Spring Point with LF in *D*, RF Fourth Intermediate Position in *B* (count ' 4 ').

Bar 4—Beginning with Spring into *A* with RF, execute four Spring Points turning over the Second Sword as in Bar 4 of the Second Step (count '5, 6, 7, 8').

Arms

First Position in Bar 1; Third Position in Bars 2 and 3, or alternatively, Third Position for the Open Pas de Basques and First Position for the Spring Points; First Position in Bar 4.

Bars 5 to 8—As for Bars 1 to 4 finishing with the Spring Points turning over the Third Sword.

Bars 9 to 12—As for Bars 1 to 4 finishing with the Spring Points turning over the Fourth Sword.

Bars 13 to 16—As for Bars 1 to 4 finishing with the Spring Points turning over the First Sword.

Note.—The Note to the Second Step applies also to this Step.

SIXTH STEP—REVERSE POINTS

Bar 1—Pas de Basque into *A* with RF, then into *D* with LF, as in Bar 1 of the Fourth Step (count '1& 2, 3& 4').

Bar 2—Spring Point with RF in *A*, LF Fourth Intermediate Position in *C* (count '5'); with quarter-turn to the right, Spring Point with LF in *C*, RF Fourth Intermediate Position in *A* (count '6'); with one-eighth turn to the right, Spring Point with RF in *C*, LF Fourth Intermediate Position in *B* (count '7'); with one-eighth turn to the right, Spring Point with LF in *B*, RF Second Position in *C* (count '8').

Bar 3—Making a half turn to the right during the bar, Open Pas de Basque with RF in *C*, LF in *D* (count '1& 2'); Open Pas de Basque with LF in *D*, RF in *C* (count '3& 4').

Bar 4—Starting with Spring into *A* on RF, execute four Spring Points turning over the Second Sword as in Bar 4 of the Second Step (count '5, 6, 7, 8').

Arms

First Position in Bar 1; Third Position in Bars 2 and 3; First Position in Bar 4.

Bars 5 to 8—As for Bars 1 to 4 finishing with the Spring Points turning over the Third Sword.

Bars 9 to 12—As for Bars 1 to 4 finishing with the Spring Points turning over the Fourth Sword.

43

Bars 13 to 16—As for Bars 1 to 4 finishing with the Spring Points turning over the First Sword.

Note.—The note to the Second Step applies also to this Step.

MUSIC CHANGES TO TEMPO 2

SEVENTH STEP—OPEN PAS DE BASQUE QUICK STEP

Bar 1—Pas de Basque into *A* with RF (count '₁& 2 ') ; Pas de Basque into *D* with LF (count '₃& 4 ').

Bar 2—Open Pas de Basque into *A* with RF, LF Fourth-opposite-Fifth Position in *B* (count '₅& 6 ') ; Open Pas de Basque with LF in *A*, RF Fourth-opposite-Fifth Position in *B* (count '₇& 8 ').

Bar 3—With quarter turn to the left on the first count, Open Pas de Basque into *B* with RF, LF Fourth-opposite-Fifth Position in *C* (count '₁& 2 ') ; Open Pas de Basque with LF in *B*, RF Fourth-opposite-Fifth Position in *C* (count '₃& 4 ').

Bar 4—Open Pas de Basque with RF in *B*, LF Fourth Intermediate Position in *D* (count '₅& 6 ') ; Open Pas de Basque into *A* with LF, RF Fourth Intermediate Position in *C* (count '₇& 8 ').

Bar 5—Open Pas de Basque into *B* with RF, LF Fourth-opposite-Fifth Position in *C* (count '₁& 2 ') ; Open Pas de Basque with LF in *B*, RF Fourth-opposite-Fifth Position in *C* (count '₃& 4 ').

Bar 6—With quarter turn to the left on the Fifth Count, Open Pas de Basque into *C* with RF, LF Fourth-opposite-Fifth Position in *D* (count '₅& 6 ') ; Open Pas de Basque with LF in *C*, RF Fourth-opposite-Fifth Position in *D* (count '₇& 8 ').

Bar 7—With quarter turn to the left on the First Count, Open Pas de Basque into *D* with RF, LF Fourth-opposite-Fifth Position in *A* (count '₁& 2 ') ; Open Pas de Basque with LF in *D*, RF Fourth-opposite-Fifth Position in *A* (count '₃& 4 ').

Bar 8—Open Pas de Basque with RF in *D*, LF Fourth Intermediate Position in *B* (count '₅& 6 ') ; Open Pas de Basque into *C* with LF, RF Fourth Intermediate Position in *A* (count '₇& 8 ').

Bar 9—Open Pas de Basque with RF into *D*, LF Fourth-opposite-Fifth Position in *A* (count '₁& 2 ') ; Open Pas de Basque with LF in *D*, RF Fourth-opposite-Fifth Position in *A* (count '₅& 6 ').

44

Bars 10 to 16—With a quarter turn to the left on the first count repeat Bars
2 to 8.

Arms

First Position in Bar 1 ; Third Position in Bars 2 to 16.

ALTERNATIVE METHOD FOR BAR 1

Open Pas de Basque with RF in *D*, LF Fourth-opposite-Fifth Position in *A*
(count ' $_1$& 2 ') ; Open Pas de Basque with LF in *D*, RF Fourth-opposite-
Fifth Position in *A* (count ' $_3$& 4 ').

Arms

Third Position.

It is now necessary to make a quarter turn to the left on beginning Bar 2.

Note.—If the Dance is to finish with this step, Bar 16 should be executed as
follows :

Execute four Back-steps in *D*, springing RF, LF, RF, LF, travelling backwards in a
curving line to 1*d* and taking *arms* down to First Position.

EIGHTH STEP—CROSSING AND POINTING QUICK-STEP

Note.—The amount of turn given for any Open Pas be Basque or Spring
Point in this Step is approximate.

Bar 1—Pas de Basque into *A* with RF (count ' $_1$& 2 ') ; Pas de Basque into
D with LF (count ' $_3$& 4 ').

Bar 2—With one-eighth turn to the left, Open Pas de Basque into *A* with
RF, LF Fourth-opposite-Fifth Position in *C* (count ' $_5$& 6 ') ; with one-
eighth turn to the left, Open Pas de Basque with LF in *A*, RF Second
Position in *B* (count ' $_7$& 8 ').

Bar 3—With one-eighth turn to the left, Open Pas de Basque into *B* with
RF, LF Fourth-opposite-Fifth Position in *D* (count ' $_1$& 2 ') ; with one-
eighth turn to the left, Open Pas de Basque with LF in *B*, RF Second
Position in *C* (count ' $_3$& 4 ').

Bar 4—With one-eighth turn to the left, Spring Point with RF in *C*, LF Fourth
Position in *A* (count ' 5 ') ; with three-eighths turn to the right, Spring
Point with LF in *A*, RF Fourth Intermediate Position in *C* (count ' 6 ') ;
with one-eighth turn to the right, Spring Point with RF in *A*, LF Fourth
Intermediate Position in *D* (count ' 7 ') ; with one-eighth turn to the
right, Spring Point with LF in *D*, RF Second Position in *A* (count ' 8 ').

45

Arms

First Position in Bar 1 ; Third Position in Bars 2 and 3 ; First Position in Bar 4.

Bars 5 and 6—Repeat Bars 2 and 3 (count ' ₁& 2, ₃& 4, ₅& 6, ₇& 8 ').

Bar 7—With one-eighth turn to the left, Open Pas de Basque with RF in *C*, LF Fourth-opposite-Fifth Position in *A* (count ' ₁& 2 ') ; with one-eighth turn to the left, Open Pas de Basque with LF in *C*, RF Second Position in *D* (count ' ₃& 4 ').

Bar 8—With one-eighth turn to the left, Spring Point with RF in *D*, LF Fourth Position in *B* (count ' 5 ') ; with three-eighths turn to the right, Spring Point with LF in *B*, RF Fourth Intermediate Position in *D* (count ' 6 ') ; with one-eighth turn to the right, Spring Point with RF in *B*, LF Fourth Intermediate Position in *A* (count ' 7 ') ; with one-eighth turn to the right, Spring Point with LF in *A*, RF Second Position in *B* (count ' 8 ').

Arms

Third Position in Bars 5, 6 and 7 ; First Position in Bar 8.

Bars 9 to 12—As for Bars 5 to 8, but begin over the Second Sword and finish over the Third Sword.

Bars 13 to 15—As for Bars 9, 10 and 11, but begin over the Third Sword and finish over the Second Sword.

Bar 16—With one-eighth turn to the left, Spring Point with RF in *B*, LF Fourth Position in *D* (count ' 5 ') ; with three-eighths turn to the right, Spring Point with LF in *D*, RF Fourth Intermediate Position in *B* (count ' 6 ' ; travelling backwards towards 1*d* spring RF, taking LF quickly to Third Aerial Position (count ' 7 ') ; execute one Back-step springing LF and finishing at 1*d* facing the front (count ' 8 ').

Arms

First Position in Bar 16.

ALTERNATIVE METHOD FOR BAR 1

Open Pas de Basque with RF in *D*, LF Fourth-opposite-Fifth Position in *A* (count ' ₁& 2 ') ; Open Pas de Basque with LF in *D*, RF Fourth-opposite-Fifth Position in *A* (count ' ₃& 4 ').

Arms

Third Position

46

It is now necessary to make a three-eighths turn to the left to begin Bar 2.

Note.—When both quicksteps are being danced, this method must be used to begin the last one.

FINISH

Step to 1 with RF and close LF to RF in First Position (flat) and Bow.

Note.—In major competitions, if only one quick step is required, the Eighth Step should be danced.

3 SEANN TRIUBHAS

A Solo Dance consisting normally of not more than eight or ten steps, the last two of which are danced to the quicker tempo.

MUSIC : ' Whistle ower the Lave o't '

Tempo 1 (Slow) : $\downarrow$ = 120 (or 30 bars to the minute).

Tempo 2 (Quick) : $\downarrow$ = 152 (or 38 bars to the minute).

Grace of movement of body and limbs, associated with precision in foot positions, is a characteristic of this dance. The full range of arm movements is employed with the steps in slower tempo, and the general impression given should be a graceful and flowing exposition of Highland Dancing.

TEMPO 1

INTRODUCTION

Bars 1 and 2—Stand as for Bow.

Bar 3—Bow (count ' 1, 2, 3, 4 ').

Bar 4—Step LF towards Second Position making one-eighth turn to the right, or pivot one-eighth turn to the right taking the weight of the body on LF (flat) (count ' 5 ') ; step RF to Fourth Rear Position (flat) to finish with LF pointed in Fourth Position (count ' 6 ') ; stand thus, taking *arms* up through Fourth Position out to Third Position (count ' 7, 8 ').

FIRST STEP—BRUSHING

During the following three bars the dancer travels forward to complete a circle to the left (anti-clockwise), finishing at the starting point facing the front.

47

Bar 1—Spring LF, then three Hops LF, executing an Outward Brush RF with each movement (count ' 1, 2, 3, 4 ').

Arms

To Fifth Position on count ' 1 ' then, with a circular action, take them upwards to Fourth Position and downwards through Third Position on counts ' 2, 3, 4 '.

Bar 2—Spring RF, executing an Outward Brush LF (count ' 5 ') ; spring LF, executing an Outward Brush RF (count ' 6 ') ; spring RF, executing an Outward Brush LF (count ' 7 ') ; spring LF, executing an Outward Brush RF (count ' 8 ').

Arms

In First Position, or as for Bar 1.

Bar 3—Spring RF, then hop RF, executing an Outward Brush LF with each movement (count ' 1, 2 ') ; spring LF, then hop LF, executing an Outward Brush RF with each movement (count ' 3, 4 ').

Arms

As for Bar 1.

Bar 4—Execute four Shuffles, springing RF, LF, RF, LF (count ' 1& 2& 3& 4& ').

Arms

First Position.

Bars 5 to 8—Repeat Bars 1 to 4 with the opposite foot but, in Bars 5 to 7, make a circle to the right (clockwise).

Note 1.—When an Outward Brush is executed in conjunction with a Hop, it is begun by taking the working foot to Third Aerial Position Low during the elevation, and finished with that foot in Fourth Aerial Position. The same also applies when an Outward Brush is executed in conjunction with a Spring, but, in the latter case only, the working foot may be brushed straight forward through First Position to Fourth Aerial Position.

Note 2.—The sequence of Outward Brushes executed with a Hop or Spring in Bars 1 to 3 and Bars 5 to 7 of this Step may be varied.

ALTERNATIVE FIRST STEP

Bars 1 to 4—As for Bars 1 to 4 of the First Step.

Bar 5—Pas de Basque RF (count ' 1 & 2 ') ; Pas de Basque LF (count ' 3 & 4 ').

Arms

First Position.

Bars 6 and 7—Repeat Bar 5 twice more (count ' 5 & 6, 7 & 8, 1 & 2, 3 & 4 ').

Bar 8—Execute four Shuffles with *arms* in First Position (count ' $_1$& $_2$& $_3$& $_4$& ').

SECOND STEP—SIDE TRAVEL

Bar 1—Spring LF (or hop LF) extending RF with Shake towards Second Aerial Position High (count ' 1 ') ; place ball of RF in Fifth Rear Position (count ' 2 ') ; step LF to Second Position, then place ball of RF in Fifth Position or Fifth Rear Position (count ' & 3 ') ; step LF to Second Position, then place ball of RF in Fifth Rear Position (count ' & 4 ').

During counts ' & 3 & 4 ' the dancer travels directly towards the left side.

Arms

To Fifth Position on count ' 1 ' then, with a circular action, take them upwards to Fourth Position and downwards through Third Position on counts ' 2, & 3 & 4 '.

Bar 2—Beginning with Hop RF, repeat Bar 1 with the opposite foot, travelling directly towards the right side (count ' 5, 6 & 7 & 8 ').

Bar 3—Beginning with Hop LF (instead of Spring), repeat Bar 1 (count ' 1, 2 & 3 & 4 ').

Bar 4—Execute four Shuffles, springing LF, RF, LF, RF, with *arms* in First Position (count ' $_5$& $_6$& $_7$& $_8$& ').

Bars 5 to 8—Beginning with Hop RF, repeat Bars 1 to 4 with the opposite foot.

THIRD STEP—DIAGONAL TRAVEL

Bar 1—Facing diagonally to the right, hop LF, with RF in Fourth Intermediate Aerial Position, then execute an Inward Brush RF to Third Aerial Position Low (count ' 1 and [and] ') ; place RF on the half point in Fifth Position, then lightly beat the ball of LF in Fifth Rear Position at the same time extending RF to Fourth Intermediate Aerial Position (count ' a 2 ') ; travelling slightly forward in a diagonal line to the right, spring RF, executing an Outward Brush LF, then Spring LF, executing an Outward Brush RF (count ' 3, 4 ').

49

Arms

Second Position on counts ' 1 and [and] a 2 ', First Position or Third Position on counts ' 3, 4 '.

Note.—The remarks in Note 1 to the First Step, concerning an Outward Brush when executed in conjunction with a Spring, apply also to this Step.

Bar 2—Repeat counts ' 1 and [and] a 2 ' of Bar 1 (Hop, Brush, beat, beat), but the extension of the working foot on count ' 2 ' may be omitted (count ' 5 and [and] a 6 ') ; execute a Pivot Turn to the left, finishing facing diagonally to the left (count ' 7, 8 ').

Arms

Second Position on counts ' 5 and [and] a 6 ', First or Fourth Position during the Pivot Turn.

Bars 3 and 4—Repeat Bars 1 and 2 with the opposite foot, travelling slightly forward in a diagonal line to the left, and turning to the right with the Pivot Turn which is finished facing diagonally to the right.

Bars 5 to 8—Repeat Bars 1 to 4, but finish facing the front.

ALTERNATIVE THIRD STEP

Bar 1—Execute Bar 1 of Third Step (count ' 1 and [and] a 2, 3, 4 ').

Bar 2—Repeat counts ' 1 and [and] a 2 ' of Bar 1 (count ' 5 and [and] a 6 ') ; two Hops LF, carrying RF with two slight Shake actions from Fourth Intermediate Aerial Position to Second Aerial Position (count ' 7 & ') ; spring RF to displace LF, which is extended to Fourth Intermediate Aerial Position (count ' 8 ').

or alternatively

Repeat counts ' 1 and [and] a 2 ' of Bar 1, but omit the extension of the working foot on the last count (count ' 5 and [and] a 6 ') ; hop LF, extending RF to Fourth Intermediate Aerial Position, then execute another Hop LF carrying RF, with a slight Shake action, to Second Aerial Position (count ' 7 & ') ; spring RF to displace LF, which is extended to Fourth Intermediate Aerial Position (count ' 8 ').

Note.—On counts ' 7 & 8 ' make a quarter turn to the left and finish facing diagonally to the left.

Arms

In Second Position, changing to Second Position on the other side on count ' 8 '.

Bars 3 and 4—Repeat Bars 1 and 2 with the opposite foot, and finish facing diagonally to the right.

Bars 5 to 8—Execute Bars 5 to 8 of the Third Step.

FOURTH STEP—BACKWARD TRAVEL

Bar 1—Repeat counts '1 and [and] a 2' of Bar 1 of the Third Step (Hop, Brush, beat, beat), but the extension of the working foot on count '2' may be omitted (count '1 and [and] a 2') ; hop LF, taking RF to Third Rear Aerial Position (count '3') ; hop LF, passing RF, as in Shedding, to Third Aerial Position (count '4').

Arms

Second Position.

Bar 2—Repeat counts '1 and [and] a 2' of Bar 1 (count '5 and [and] a 6') ; two Hops LF, carrying RF, with two slight Shake actions from Fourth Intermediate Aerial Position to Second Aerial Position (count '7 & ') ; spring RF to displace LF, which is extended to Fourth Intermediate Aerial Position (count '8').

or alternatively

Repeat counts '1 and [and] a 2' of Bar 1, but omit the extension of the working foot on the last count (count '5 and [and] a 6') ; hop LF, extending RF to Fourth Intermediate Aerial Position, then execute another Hop LF, carrying RF, with a slight Shake action, to Second Aerial Position (count '7 & ') ; spring RF to displace LF, which is extended to Fourth Intermediate Aerial Position (count '8').

Arms

Second Position, changing to Second Position on the other side on count '8'.

Bars 3 and 4—Repeat Bars 1 and 2 with the opposite foot.

Bars 5 to 8—Repeat Bars 1 to 4.

Note.—During the above step, gradually move backwards to original position.

ALTERNATIVE FOURTH STEP

(Usually danced if the alternative Third Step is used)

Bar 1—Execute Bar 2 of the Fourth Step (count '1 and [and] a 2, 3 & 4').

Bar 2—Repeat Bar 1 with the opposite foot (count '5 and [and] a 6, 7 & 8').

51

Bar 3—Repeat Bar 1 (count ' 1 and [and] a 2, 3 & 4 ').

Bar 4—Execute four Shuffles, beginning with spring LF (count ' ₅& ₆& ₇& ₈& ').

Arms

Second Position in Bars 1, 2 and 3 ; First Position in Bar 4.

Bars 5 to 8—Repeat Bars 1 to 4 with the opposite foot.

Note.—During Bars 1 to 3 and 5 to 7, gradually move backwards to original position.

FIFTH STEP—TRAVELLING BALANCE

Bar 1—Execute the Balance movement, springing RF, LF (count ' 1, 2 ') ; spring RF to displace LF, which is taken to Third Rear Aerial Position (count ' 3 ') ; pass LF, as in Shedding, to Third Aerial Position then hop RF, extending LF to Fourth Intermediate Aerial Position (count ' & 4 ').

Arms

Third Position.

Bar 2—Execute the Travelling Balance movement, beginning with LF (count ' 5 & 6, 7 & 8 ').

Bars 3 and 4—Repeat Bars 1 and 2 with the opposite foot.

Bars 5 to 8—Repeat Bars 1 to 4.

Note.—If the Sixth Step is to follow, there is no extension of the foot on the last count of the above step, the feet remaining in Fifth Position.

SIXTH STEP—LEAP AND HIGH CUT

Note.—This step should follow a step which may be finished with the weight of the body equally distributed on the balls of both feet in Third or Fifth Position.

Bar 1—Leap, landing with RF in front (count ' 1 ') ; disassemble with High Cut RF (count ' ₂& ') ; hop LF, passing RF, as in Shedding, to Third Aerial Position (count ' 3 ') ; place RF on the half point in Fifth Position, then lightly beat ball of LF in Fifth Rear Position, extending RF to Fourth Intermediate Aerial Position Low (count ' & 4 ').

Arms

Take arms to Fourth Position on count ' 1 ', changing to Second Position on count ' 2 '.

52

Bar 2—Execute three Shuffles, springing RF, LF, RF (count '$_5$& $_6$& $_7$& ') ; beginning with LF, execute the elevation as for Shuffle but assemble landing with RF in front in Fifth Position (count ' 8 ').

Arms

First Position.

Note.—On counts ' & 4 ' in Bar 1, the working foot may be placed on the half point towards Fourth Intermediate Position, then the other foot closed to Fifth Rear Position, in which case, to regain starting line, the dancer travels slightly backwards while executing the Shuffles in Bar 2.

Bars 3 and 4—Repeat Bars 1 and 2 with the opposite foot.

Bars 5 to 8—Repeat Bars 1 to 4.

Alternative Sixth Step—Leap and Shedding

Bar 1—Leap, landing with LF in front (count ' 1 ') ; disassemble, taking RF to Third Rear Aerial Position (count ' 2 ') ; hop LF, passing RF, as in Shedding, to Third Aerial Position (count ' 3 ') ; place RF on the half point towards Fourth Intermediate Position, then close ball of LF to Fifth Rear Position extending RF to Fourth Intermediate Aerial Position Low (count ' & 4 ').

Arms

First Position on count ' 1 ', raise arms up at sides through Third Position to Fourth Position on counts ' 2, 3, & 4 '.

Bar 2—Execute Bar 2 of the Sixth Step with slight backward travel to regain starting line (count ' $_5$& $_6$& $_7$& 8 ').

Arms

On counts '$_5$& $_6$& $_7$& ' take arms down at sides through Third Position to arrive in First Position on count ' 8 '.

Bars 3 and 4—Repeat Bars 1 and 2 with the opposite foot.

Bars 5 to 8—Repeat Bars 1 to 4.

SEVENTH STEP—HIGH CUT IN FRONT AND BALANCE

Bar 1—Hop (or spring) LF, with High Cut in front RF (count ' 1 and [and] ') ; place RF on the half point towards Fourth Intermediate Position (count ' a ') ; close LF to Fifth Rear Position, extending RF to Fourth Intermediate Aerial Position (count ' 2 ') ; execute the Balance movement, springing RF, LF (count ' 3, 4 ').

Arms

Second Position on counts ' 1 and [and] a 2 ' ; Third Position on counts ' 3, 4 ').

Bar 2—Repeat counts ' 1 and [and] a 2 ' of Bar 1 (count ' 5 and [and] a 6 ') ; spring RF, taking LF to Third Rear Aerial Position (count ' 7 ') ; hop RF, passing LF, as in Shedding, to Third Aerial Position (count ' 8 ').

Arms

Second Position on counts ' 5 and [and] a 6 ' changing to Second Position on the other side on count ' 7 '.

Bars 3 and 4—Repeat Bars 1 and 2 with the other foot.

Bars 5 to 8—Repeat Bars 1 to 4.

ALTERNATIVE SEVENTH STEP

Bars 1 to 3—Execute Bars 1 to 3 of the Seventh Step.

Bar 4—Execute four Shuffies, springing LF, RF, LF, RF, as in Bar 4 of the Second Step.

Bars 5 to 8—Repeat Bars 1 to 4 with the opposite foot.

EIGHTH STEP—SIDE HEEL-AND-TOE

Bar 1—Hop (or spring) LF, extending RF towards Second Aerial Position during the elevation and taking it inwards to Third Aerial or Third Rear Aerial Position simultaneously on landing (count ' 1 ') ; place heel of RF towards Second Position, then, momentarily taking the weight on that heel, place the ball of LF in Fifth Rear Position, allowing the knee of the right leg to relax (count ' & 2 ') ; place RF on the half point towards Second Position, then place ball of LF in Fifth Rear Position (count ' & 3 ') ; place heel of RF towards Second Position then close ball of LF to Fifth Rear Position as before (count ' & 4 ').

Arms

Second Position.

Note.—During this Bar the dancer travels directly towards the right side.

Bar 2—Execute Bar 2 of the Fourth Step (count ' 5 and [and] a 6, 7 & 8 ').

Bars 3 and 4—Beginning with Hop RF, repeat Bars 1 and 2 with the opposite foot, travelling directly towards the left side back to starting point.

Bars 5 to 8—Beginning with Hop LF, repeat Bars 1 to 4 but a Pivot Turn to the left may be executed on counts ' 7, 8 ' in Bar 6, in which case a Pivot Turn to the right is executed on counts ' 7, 8 ' in Bar 8.

NINTH STEP—DOUBLE HIGH CUTTING

Note.—There is no travel in this step.

Bar 1—Execute counts ' 1 and [and] a 2 ' of Bar 1 of the Third Step (Hop, Brush, beat, beat) (count ' 1 and [and] a 2 ') ; hop LF, with High Cut RF (count ' $_3$& ') ; hop LF, with High Cut in Front RF (count ' $_4$& ').

Bar 2—Repeat counts ' 1 and [and] a 2 ' of Bar 1 (count ' 5 and [and] a 6 ') ; spring RF, with High Cut LF (count ' $_7$& ') ; hop RF, with High Cut in Front LF (count ' $_8$ &').

Arms

Second Position, changing to the other side on count ' 7 '.

Bars 3 and 4—Repeat Bars 1 and 2 with the opposite foot.

Bars 5 to 8—Repeat Bars 1 to 4.

MUSIC CHANGES TO TEMPO 2

TENTH STEP—SHEDDING WITH BACK-STEP

Bar 1—Hop LF, pointing RF in Second Position (count ' 1 ') ; hop LF, taking RF to Third Rear Aerial Position (count ' 2 ') ; hop LF, passing RF, as in Shedding, to Third Aerial Position (count ' 3 ') ; execute one Back-step with RF (count ' 4 ').

Arms

Second Position, changing to the other side on count ' 4 '.

Bar 2—Repeat Bar 1 with the opposite foot (count ' 5, 6, 7, 8 ').

Bar 3—Repeat Bar 1 (count ' 1, 2, 3, 4 ').

Bar 4—Hop RF, pointing LF in Second Position (count ' 5 ') ; turn to the right as in Bar 4 of the First Highland Fling Step (count ' 6, 7, 8 ').

Bars 5 to 8—Repeat Bars 1 to 4 with the opposite foot and turning to the left on Bar 8.

ELEVENTH STEP—TOE-AND-HEEL, AND ROCK

Bar 1—Spring LF, then hop LF (or two Hops LF if required), executing the Toe-and-Heel movement in Second Position with RF (count ' 1, 2 ') ; two Hops LF, executing the Toe-and-Heel movement in Fifth Position with RF (count ' 3, 4 ').

Arms

Second Position.

Bar 2—Execute four Rocks, springing RF, LF, RF, LF (count ' 5, 6, 7, 8 ').

Arms

Third position.

Bars 3 and 4—Repeat Bars 1 and 2 with the opposite foot.

Bars 5 to 8—Repeat Bars 1 to 4.

TWELFTH STEP—POINTING AND BACK-STEPPING

Bar 1—Hop (or spring if required) LF, pointing RF in Fourth Position (count ' 1 ') ; hop LF, taking RF to Third Aerial Position (count ' 2 ') ; hop LF, pointing RF in Fourth Position (count ' 3 ') ; take RF sharply to Third Aerial Position then spring, displacing LF, which is taken sharply to Third Rear Aerial Position (count ' 4 ').

Arms

Second Position, changing to the other side on count 4.

Bar 2—Repeat Bar 1 with the opposite foot (count ' 5, 6, 7, 8 ').

Bar 3—Repeat Bar 1 (count ' 1, 2, 3, 4 ').

Bar 4—Execute four Back-steps, springing LF, RF, LF, RF (count ' 5, 6, 7, 8 ').

Arms

Third Position.

Note.—The Back-stepping in Bar 4 is begun from Third Rear Aerial Position.

Bars 5 to 8—Repeat Bars 1 to 4 with the opposite foot.

THIRTEENTH STEP—HEEL-AND-TOE AND SHEDDING

Bar 1—Hop (or spring) LF, pointing RF in Second Position (count ' 1 ') ; hop LF, taking RF to Third Rear Aerial Position (count ' 2 ') ; execute the Heel-and-Toe movement with RF (count ' 3, 4 ').

Bar 2—Beginning with Hop, instead of Disassemble, execute Bar 1 (Shedding) of the First Highland Fling Step (count '5, 6, 7, 8 ').

Arms
Second Position in Bars 1 and 2.

Bars 3 and 4—Beginning with Spring RF, repeat Bars 1 and 2 with the opposite foot.

Bars 5 to 8—Beginning with Spring LF, repeat Bars 1 to 4.

FOURTEENTH STEP—HEEL-AND-TOE, SHEDDING, AND BACK-STEPPING

Bars 1 and 2—Execute Bars 1 and 2 of the Thirteenth Step.

Bar 3—Execute four Back-steps, springing RF, LF, RF, LF (count ' 1, 2, 3, 4 ').

Bar 4—Turn to the right as in Bar 4 of the First Highland Fling Step (count ' 5, 6, 7, 8 ').

Arms
Second Position in Bars 1 and 2 ; Third Position in Bar 3 ; First or Second Position in Bar 4.

Bars 5 to 8—Repeat Bars 1 to 4 with the opposite foot, turning to the left on Bar 8.

Note.—If the above is used as a last step, Bars 7 and 8 may be executed as follows :

Hop LF, pointing RF in Second Position (count ' 1 ') ; execute two turns to the left as in Bars 7 and 8 of the Eighth Highland Fling Step (count ' 2, 3, 4, 5, 6, 7, 8 ').

FIFTEENTH STEP—BACK-STEPPING

Bar 1—Hop LF, pointing RF in Second Position (count ' 1 ') ; hop LF, taking RF to Third Rear Aerial Position (count ' 2 ') ; execute two Back-steps, springing RF, LF, and finish with RF in Third Aerial Position (count ' 3, 4 ').

Arms
Second Position on counts ' 1, 2 ' ; Third Position on counts ' 3, 4 '.

Bar 2—Starting with Spring (instead of Hop), repeat Bar 1 with the opposite foot (count ' 5, 6, 7, 8 ').

Bar 3—Starting with Spring (instead of Hop), repeat Bar 1 (count ' 1, 2, 3, 4 ').

Bar 4—Turn to the right as in the fourth bar of the First Step of the Highland Fling (count ' 5, 6, 7, 8 ').

Bars 5 to 8—Repeat Bars 1 to 4 with the opposite foot.

SIXTEENTH STEP

Dance the Third Step of the Highland Fling (Toe-and-Heel).

SEVENTEENTH STEP

Dance the Fourth Step of the Highland Fling (Rocking).

EIGHTEENTH STEP

Dance the Eighth Step of the Highland Fling (Last Shedding). This step can be used only as a last step.

PREPARATION FOR THE FINISH

Method 1

On the last bar of the final step of the Dance assemble with LF in front (count ' 5 ') ; leap, landing with RF in front (count ' 6, 7 ') ; pause (count ' 8 ').

Method 2

On the fourth count of the seventh bar of the final step of the Dance, assemble with RF in front (count ' 4 '), then execute Bar 8 as follows :
Leap, landing with LF in front (count ' 5, 6 ') ; leap, landing with change of foot (count ' 7, 8 ').

Method 3

Execute two turns to the left as in the Eighth Highland Fling Step (see Eighteenth Step and note to Fourteenth Step).

FINISH

Step to the right with RF, then close LF to RF in First Position (flat) and bow.

4 STRATHSPEY

A Dance performed by four Dancers.

MUSIC : Any Strathspey Tune.

Tempo : ♩ = 152 (or 38 bars to the minute).

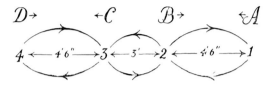

INTRODUCTION

As shown in the diagram, the four dancers, A, B, C and D, stand in a straight line at points 1, 2, 3 and 4 respectively.   A and B are facing each other, C and D are also facing each other.

Bars 1 and 2—All stand as for Bow (8 counts).

Bars 3 and 4—All bow (count ' 1, 2, 3, 4 ') ; all swivel one-eighth turn to the left, taking *arms* to First Position if not already in that position (count ' 5, 6') ; point RF in Fourth Position (count ' 7 ') ; turn the body at an angle of 45° to the line of travel for the Figure of Eight (right shoulder leading), taking RF to Third Aerial Position and *arms* to Third Position (count ' 8 ').

Note 1.—The point on count ' 7 ' may be omitted.

Note 2.—The dancers may rise on the ball of the LF on count ' 8 '.

FIRST STEP

FIGURE OF EIGHT

Bars 1 to 7—Moving forward along the line of travel, as indicated by the arrows in the diagram, each dancer executes seven Progressive Strathspey Movements.   Dancers A and D return to their starting positions at points 1 and 4 respectively ; B and C, when approaching each other on the seventh bar, make approximately a three-eighths turn to the right, so that C finishes at point 2 facing A, and B at point 3 facing D.   On the last count of the seventh Progressive Strathspey movement the Hop on RF may be omitted and the LF extended to Second Aerial Position.

When A and D are passing each other in the centre, C and B are passing through the outer points, and vice versa.

Arms

Third Position throughout.

Bar 8—Taking *arms* to First Position, assemble with LF in front (count ' 1 ') ; leap, landing with RF in front (count ' 2, 3 ') ; pause (count ' 4 ').

SETTING

Bars 9 to 16—All dance a Highland Fling Step, e.g. the Fourth (Rocking) Step.

SECOND STEP

FIGURE OF EIGHT

Bars 1 to 8—As for Bars 1 to 8 of the First Step with B and C finishing in their original positions at points 2 and 3 respectively.

SETTING

Bars 9 to 16—All dance a Highland Fling Step, e.g. the Sixth (Cross-over) Step.

The First Step or the First and Second Steps may be repeated using a different Highland Fling Step each time. The Strathspey is usually followed by a Reel, but if not, all dancers face the front after the last setting step, then bow.

Note 1.—As will be seen from the diagram, with reference to the line of travel, the term ' Figure of Eight ' is a misnomer, but the name has been retained because it is traditional.

Note 2.—If the Second or Fifth Steps of the Highland Fling are used (both of which finish with Back-stepping) then, on the last count of the step, hop LF, keeping RF in Third Aerial Position, ready to recommence the Figure of Eight. N.B.—Similarly if the Fourth Step of the Highland Fling is used (which finishes with Rocking), on the last two counts of the step spring LF, taking RF to Third Rear Aerial Position (count ' 7 '), then hop LF, passing RF, as in Shedding, to Third Aerial Position (count ' 8 ') or alternatively, on the last count of the step hop LF, taking RF to Third Aerial Position.

Note 3.—If the Strathspey is to be followed by the complete Reel of Tulloch an even number of Strathspey steps should be danced, so that the dancers are in their original position to begin the Reel.

Note 4.—Bar 1 of all Highland Fling Steps used for setting will begin with Disassemble instead of Hop or Spring.

Note 5.—On the last two beats of a Setting step the dancers should make a one-eighth turn to the left preparatory to starting the Figure of Eight.

5 HIGHLAND REEL

This dance usually follows the Strathspey with the music changing to Reel Time without any break between the dances.

MUSIC : Any Scottish Reel Tune.

Tempo : $\quad$ = 132 or 66 Bars to the minute (count two in the bar).

Note 1.—During the Highland Reel the distance between the points may be reduced.

Note 2.—On the last two beats of a Setting step the dancers should make a one-eighth turn to the left preparatory to starting the Figure of Eight.

FIRST STEP

FIGURE OF EIGHT

Bars 1 to 8—The dancers follow the same line of travel, and begin and finish at the same points as described in Part 1 of the First Step in the Strathspey, but eight Progressive Reel Movements are danced to complete the Figure of Eight.

Arms

Third Position throughout.

or alternatively

Execute seven Progressive Reel Movements with *arms* in Third Position (7 bars) ; assemble with LF in front, taking *arms* to First Position, then change (1 bar).

If this method is used, a Basic Reel Step which is described as beginning with Hop will instead begin with Disassemble and, for a Basic Reel Step described as beginning with Assemble or the Balance movement, preparation is made on the last count of the bar preceeding that on which the Basic Reel Step begins, by extending the RF towards Second Aerial Position Low or to Fourth Intermediate Aerial Position.

SETTING

Bars 9 to 16—All dance a Basic Reel Step.

SECOND STEP

FIGURE OF EIGHT

Bars 1 to 8—As for the First Step, but the dancers finish as for the Second Step of the Strathspey.

SETTING

Bars 9 to 16—All dance a Basic Reel Step.

The First, or the First and Second Steps may be repeated using a different Basic Reel Step each time.

When setting for the last time all dancers either (*a*) execute sixteen High Cuts making one turn to the right on the spot, or (*b*) execute four Bars of the same Basic Reel Step, then execute eight High Cuts making one turn to the right on the spot, to finish facing partner in both cases.

FINISH

All step to the right with RF, close LF to RF in First Position (flat) of the feet, then bow to partner. All step with LF into line facing the front, close RF to LF in First Position (flat) of the feet, then bow to audience.

6 BASIC REEL STEPS

FIRST STEP—SHAKE AND TRAVEL

Bar 1—Hop LF, pointing RF in Fifth Position (count ' 1 ') ; hop LF, extending RF with Shake to Second Aerial Position (count ' 2 ').

Bar 2—Hop LF, then close ball of RF to Fifth Rear Position (count ' &3') ; step LF to Second Position, then close ball of RF to Fifth Position (count ' & 4 ').

Arms

Second Position, changing to Second Position on the other side on count & 4.

Bars 3 and 4—Repeat Bars 1 and 2 with the opposite foot (count ' 5, 6 &7 & 8 ').

Bars 5 and 6—Repeat Bars 1 and 2 (count ' 1, 2 &3 & 4 ').

Bars 7 and 8—Execute two High Cuts, springing LF, RF (count ' 5 & 6 & ') ; spring LF, taking RF as for High Cut to Third Rear Aerial Position, then pass RF, as in Shedding, to Third Aerial Position (count ' 7 & ') ; hop LF with High Cut RF (count ' 8 & ').

Arms

Third Position.

ALTERNATIVE METHOD

Bars 1 to 4—Execute Bars 1 to 4 as described above (count ' 1, 2 &3 & 4, 5, 6 &7 8 ').

Bars 5 to 8—Execute eight High Cuts with Spring, beginning with Spring RF (count ' 1 & 2 & 3 & 4 & 5 & 6 & 7 & 8 & ').

Arms

Third Position.

SECOND STEP—BALANCE AND PAS DE BASQUE

Bar 1—Execute the Balance movement, springing RF, LF (count ' 1, 2 ').

Bar 2—Pas de Basque RF (count ' 3 & 4 ')

Arms

Third Position in Bar 1, First Position in Bar 2.

Bars 3 and 4—Repeat Bars 1 and 2 with the opposite foot (count ' 5, 6, 7 & 8 ').

Bars 5 to 8—Repeat Bars 1 to 4.

First Alternative Method

Bars 1 to 6—Execute Bars 1 to 6, as described above.

Bars 7 and 8—Execute Bars 7 and 8 of the First Step.

Second Alternative Method

Bars 1 to 4—Execute Bars 1 to 4 as described above.

Bars 5 to 8—Execute Bars 5 to 8 of the First Step Alternative Method.

THIRD STEP—BRUSHING

Bar 1—Hop LF, executing an Outward Brush with RF from Third Aerial Position Low to Fourth Aerial Position (count ' 1 ') ; repeat Hop LF, with Outward Brush RF (count ' 2 ').

Bar 2—Spring RF, executing an Outward Brush with LF from Third Aerial Position Low to Fourth Aerial Position (count ' 3 ') ; hop RF, repeating the Outward Brush LF (count ' 4 ').

Bars 3 and 4—Execute four High Cuts, springing LF, RF, LF, RF (count ' 5 & 6 & 7 & 8 & ').

Arms

Second Position in Bars 1 and 2 ; Third Position in Bars 3 and 4.

Bars 5 to 8—Repeat Bars 1 to 4 with the opposite foot.

63

FOURTH STEP—HIGH CUTS AND SPRING POINTS

Bar 1—Execute two High Cuts, springing RF, LF (count ' 1 & 2 & ').

Bar 2—Execute two Spring Points, springing RF, LF, with the working foot in Fourth Position each time (count ' 3, 4 ').

Arms
Third Position in Bar 1 ; First Position in Bar 2.

Bars 3 to 6—Repeat Bars 1 and 2 twice more (count ' 5 & 6 & 7, 8, 1 & 2 & 3, 4).

Bars 7 and 8—Execute four High Cuts, springing RF, LF, RF, LF, with arms in Third Position (count ' 5 & 6 & 7 & 8 & ').

FIFTH STEP—BALANCE AND ROUND-THE-LEG

Bar 1—Execute the Balance movement, springing RF, LF (count ' 1, 2 ').

Bar 2—Spring RF, taking LF to Third Rear Aerial Position, then pass LF, as in Shedding, to Third Aerial Position (count ' 3 & ') ; hop RF, extending LF to Fourth Intermediate Aerial Position (count ' 4 ').

Bars 3 and 4—Repeat Bars 1 and 2 with the opposite foot (count ' 5, 6, 7 & 8 ').

Bar 5—Repeat Bar 2 (count ' 1 & 2 ').

Bar 6—Repeat Bar 5 with the opposite foot (count ' 3 & 4 ').

Bars 7 and 8—Execute four High Cuts as in Bar 8 of the Fourth Step (count ' 5 & 6 & 7 & 8 & ').

Arms
Third Position throughout.

ALTERNATIVE METHOD

Bars 1 to 4—Execute Bars 1 to 4 as described above.

Bars 5 and 6—Repeat Bars 1 and 2.

Bars 7 and 8—Execute Bars 7 and 8 of the First Step.

SIXTH STEP—BACK-STEP AND TRAVEL

Bar 1—Take RF sharply to Third Aerial Position and execute one Back-step (count ' 1 ') ; place LF on the half point towards Second Position (count ' & ') ; place ball of RF in Fifth Rear Position, extending LF to Fourth Intermediate Aerial Position (count ' 2 ') ; take LF to Third Rear Aerial Position (count ' & ').

Bar 2—Spring LF with High Cut RF (count ' 3 & ') ; spring RF, taking LF as for High Cut to Third Rear Aerial Position (count ' 4 ') ; pass LF as in Shedding, to Third Aerial Position (count ' & ').

Bars 3 and 4—Repeat Bars 1 and 2 with the opposite foot (count ' 5 & 6 & 7 & 8 & ').

Bars 5 to 8—Repeat Bars 1 to 4.

Arms

Third Position throughout.

FIRST ALTERNATIVE METHOD

Bars 1 to 6—Execute Bars 1 to 6 as described above.

Bars 7 and 8—Execute Bars 7 and 8 of the First Step.

SECOND ALTERNATIVE METHOD

Bars 1 to 4—Execute Bars 1 to 4 as described above.

Bars 5 to 8—Execute Bars 5 to 8 of the First Step alternative method (8 High Cuts).

SEVENTH STEP—ASSEMBLE AND TRAVEL

Bar 1—Assemble with LF in front (count ' 1 ') ; disassemble, taking RF to Third Rear Aerial Position (count ' 2 ').

Arms

First Position on count ' 1 ', Second Position on count ' 2 '.

Bar 2—Hop LF, passing RF, as in Shedding, to Third Aerial Position (count ' 3 ') ; place RF on the half point towards Fourth Intermediate Position (count ' & ') ; close ball of LF to Fifth Rear Position, extending RF to Fourth Intermediate Aerial Position (count ' 4 ').

Arms

Second Position.

Bars 3 and 4—Repeat Bars 1 and 2 with the opposite foot (count ' 5, 6, 7 & 8 ').

Bars 5 and 6—Repeat Bars 1 and 2 (count ' 1, 2, 3 & 4 ').

Bars 7 and 8—Execute four High Cuts springing RF, LF, RF, LF, with *arms* in Third Position (count ' 5 & 6 & 7 & 8 & ').

EIGHTH STEP—HIGH CUT IN FRONT AND BALANCE

Bar 1—Hop LF, with High Cut in Front RF (count ' 1 and [and] ') ; place RF on the half point in Fifth Position, then lightly beat the ball of LF in Fifth Rear Position, at the same time extending RF to Fourth Intermediate Aerial Position (count ' a 2 ').

Arms

Second Position.

Bar 2—Execute the Balance movement, springing RF, LF (count ' 3, 4 ').

Arms

Third Position.

Bar 3—Repeat Bar 1 (count ' 5 and [and] a 6 ').

Bar 4—Spring RF, taking LF to Third Rear Aerial Position (count ' 7 ') ; hop RF, passing LF, as in Shedding, to Third Aerial Position (count ' 8 ').

Arms

Second Position.

Bars 5 to 8—Repeat Bars 1 to 4 with the opposite foot.

ALTERNATIVE METHOD

Bars 1 to 6—Execute Bars 1 to 6 as described above.

Bars 7 and 8—Execute Bars 7 and 8 of the First Step.

NINTH STEP—SHUFFLE

Bar 1—Assemble with RF in front (count ' 1 ') ; disassemble, taking LF to Third Rear Aerial Position (count ' 2 ').

Arms

First Position on count ' 1 ', Second Position on count ' 2 '.

Bar 2—Hop RF, passing LF, as in Shedding, to Third Aerial Position (count ' 3 ') ; place LF on the half point towards Fourth Intermediate Position, then close ball of RF to Fifth Rear Position, at the same time extending LF to Fourth Intermediate Aerial Position Low (count ' & 4 ').

Arms

Second Position.

66

Bars 3 and 4—Beginning with Spring LF, execute four Shuffles with arms in First Position (count ' 5 & 6 & 7 & 8 & ').

Bars 5 to 8—Repeat Bars 1 to 4 with the opposite foot.

7 REEL OF TULLOCH OR 'HULLACHAN'

MUSIC : ' Reel of Tulloch '

Tempo : $\quad$ = 132 or 66 Bars to the Minute (count two in a bar).

This dance usually follows the Strathspey as an alternative to the Highland Reel, in which case the dancers start in the same position as for the Strathspey, namely A and B facing each other at points 1 and 2 respectively ; C and D facing each other at points 3 and 4 respectively.

PART I

Bars 1 and 2—All execute two Pas de Basque (RF then LF), travelling to finish with dancers A and D facing each other at points 2 and 3 respectively, and dancers B and C facing inwards at points 1 and 4 respectively, all keeping to the left as they pass (count ' 1 & 2, 3 & 4 ').

Note.—Dancers B and C may alternatively execute two Progressive Reel Movements with arms in Third Position (count ' &1 & 2, &3 & 4 ').

Bars 3 and 4—Dancers A and D execute two Pas de Basque (RF then LF), making one complete turn to the right (count ' 5 & 6, 7 & 8 '). Dancers B and C stand in First Position (flat) for the remainder of Part I.

Bars 5 and 6—Dancers A and D execute a Pas de Basque with RF (count ' 1 & 2 '); assemble with RF in front (count ' 3 ') ; disassemble, taking RF to Third Rear Aerial Position, having extended that foot towards Second Aerial Position during the elevation ; (the LF may also be extended towards Second Aerial Position during the elevation) (count ' 4 ').

Bars 7 and 8—Dancers A and D execute four High Cuts, springing RF, LF, RF, LF (count ' 5 & 6 & 7 & 8 & ').

Arms

Dancers A and D First Position until the first count in Bar 6, then change to Third Position on the second count of that Bar. Dancers B and C First Position throughout (but see Note at end of Bars 1 and 2).

Bars 9 to 11—A and D dance the Propelled Pivot Turn to the right, making approximately one and a half turns, finishing in a direct line with C and B (count ' 1 & 2 & 3 & 4 & 5 & 6 ').

67

Bar 12—Relinquishing the arm hold, execute two High Cuts springing LF, RF, and making approximately a half turn to the right (count ' 7 & 8 & ').

Arms

Third Position.

Bars 13 to 16—A and D dance the Propelled Pivot Turn to the left, making approximately one and three-quarters turns (count ' 1 & 2 & 3 & 4 & 5 & 6 & 7 '). Relinquishing the arm hold on the count of ' 7 ' continue the movement to finish with A at point 3 facing C, and D at point 2 facing B (count ' & 8 ').

PART 2

(Starts C→   ←A   D→   ←B)

Bars 1 to 8—All dance a Basic Reel Step.

Bars 9 to 16—B with D and A with C dance the Propelled Pivot Turn to the right, then to the left, as described in Bars 9 to 16 of Part 1, finishing with B and C facing each other at points 2 and 3 respectively, and with D and A facing inwards at points 1 and 4 respectively.

Note.—While executing the two High Cuts turning to the right to change direction, the four dancers should be in line.

PART 3

(Starts A→   C→ ←B   ←D)

Bars 1 to 8—B and C dance a Basic Reel Step.

Bars 9 to 16—B and C dance the Propelled Pivot Turn to the right, then to the left, as described in Part 1, B finishing at point 3 facing A, and C finishing at point 2 facing D. A and D stand for the above 16 bars in First Position of the feet, arms and head.

PART 4

(Starts A→   ←B   C→   ←D)

Bars 1 to 8—All dance a Basic Reel Step.

Bars 9 to 16—A with B and C with D dance the Propelled Pivot Turn to the right, then to the left, as described in Part 2, finishing with D and A facing each other at points 2 and 3 respectively, and B and C facing inwards at points 4 and 1 respectively.

PART 5

(Starts B →   A → ← D   ← C)

Bars 1 to 16—D and A dance as described for B and C in Part 3, finishing with D at point 3 facing B and with A at point 2 facing C.
    B and C stand throughout in First Position of the feet, arms and head.

PART 6

(Starts B →   ← D   A →   ← C)

Bars 1 to 16—All dance as for Part 2 finishing with C and B facing each other at points 2 and 3 respectively and with A and D facing inwards at points 1 and 4 respectively.

PART 7

(Starts D →   B → ← C   ← A)

Bars 1 to 16—As for Part 3, but B and C finish in starting positions.

PART 8

(Starts D →   ← C   B →   ← A)

Bars 1 to 8—All execute 16 High Cuts slowly making one turn to the right on the spot and finish as at the start, i.e. A facing B, C facing D.

Bars 9 to 16—A with B and C with D dance the Propelled Pivot Turn to the right then to the left as before but finish C, D, A, B, facing the front at points 4, 3, 2, 1, respectively.

FINISH

All stand in First Position (flat) of the feet and bow.

Note 1—When begun from First Position of the feet, a Basic Reel Step which is described as beginning with Hop will instead begin with Disassemble and, for a Basic Reel Step described as beginning with Assemble or the Balance movement, preparation is made on the last count of the Bar preceding that on which the Basic Reel Step begins, by extending the right foot towards Second Aerial Position Low or to the Fourth Intermediate Aerial Position.

Note 2—On the last two beats of a Setting Step the dancers should make a one-eighth turn to the left, preparatory to starting the Propelled Pivot Turn.

When the *Reel of Tulloch* is performed as a separate dance, the dancers begin as shown in the diagram.

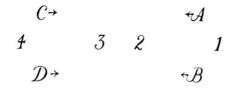

A slightly forward and inward from point 1, facing C, who is slightly forward and inward from point 4 ; B slightly back and inward from point 1, facing D, who is slightly back and inward from point 4.

INTRODUCTION

Bars 1 and 2—A and D, making a quarter turn to the left, take a short step with RF towards C and B respectively, while B and C, making a quarter turn to the right, take a short step with LF towards D and A respectively. All close in First Position (flat) of the feet facing partner, and bow (count ' 1, 2, 3, 4 ').

Bars 3 and 4—Beginning with the opposite foot, all return to starting position and acknowledge the dancer opposite with a modified Bow (count '5, 6, 7, 8')

A and D follow the dance description as given, but B and C, on the first bar, step with RF to points 1 and 4 respectively, and close LF to RF in First Position (flat) still facing inwards and stand thus for the remaining 15 bars.

Chapter Three

RUDIMENTS OF MUSIC

Teachers and students should be conversant with the following musical terms and their definitions :

Staff

The five parallel lines and the four spaces between them upon, or in which the notes of the music are depicted.

Bar

The Staff is divided by perpendicular lines called Bar-lines, into short sections of equal value in the sense that each section takes the same period of time to play. The portion of music between any two consecutive Bar-lines is termed a Bar, which is itself divided into equal portions called Beats.

Beat

One of the regular pulsations of the music, or one of the equal sub-divisions of a Bar.

Time

The maintaining of a regular, or equal interval between Beats.

Tempo

The speed at which the music is played, denoted either by the number of bars to the minute, or by a number giving the metronome time.

Accent

The emphasis placed on any particular beat. There are three accents in music, namely Strong, Medium and Weak. The strong accent occurs only once in each bar, and always on the first beat of the bar.

Rhythm

The regular or periodical recurrence of accents.

Notation

The notes most generally used in music suitable for dancing are :

| Semibreve | Minim | Crotchet | Quaver | Semi-quaver |

The value of each of these notes is half the value of the preceding note, in the order given above, thus, taking the Semi-breve as a standard, a Minim is half, a Crotchet a quarter, a Quaver an eighth, and a Semi-quaver a sixteenth of its value.

Time Signature

The indication, at the beginning of the music, or any portion of the music, which denotes the number of beats in each bar, and their value as a fraction of a Semi-breve. When figures are used, the top figure gives the number of beats in the bar, and the bottom figure their fractional value (see Notation).

Repeats

(*a*) The letters D.C., placed below the Staff under a double bar-line, indicate to the musician to return, from that point, to the beginning of the music ; the letters D.S., when similarly placed, instruct the musician to return to the point in the music denoted by the sign ·⅜· .

(*b*) When a double bar-line is followed by two or four dots in the spaces of the staff, and the next double bar-line is preceded by two or four dots similarly placed, then the portion of music between these double bars is repeated.

COUNTING OF HIGHLAND DANCING STEPS OR MOVEMENTS TO MUSIC

It is essential that both the teacher and the student should understand the method of counting steps and movements to music, using the standard rhythms explained below, all of which refer to Common Time, since Strathspey and Reel tunes used for Highland Dancing are usually written with that time signature.

Note.—In Common Time, which is denoted by the letter C on the staff, there are four crotchets in the bar, the accents being : Strong, Weak, Medium, Weak. Common Time is the same as $\frac{4}{4}$ time.

Single Beat Rhythm

Gives one sound in the space of time occupied by one beat. Thus there are four single beats in a bar of music (each represented by a crotchet) and counted :

1, 2, 3, 4

Half-Beat Rhythm

Gives two sounds of equal value in the space of time occupied by a single beat in the music. Thus there are eight half-beats in a bar (each represented by a quaver) and counted :

1 & 2 & 3 & 4 &

Imperfect Half-Beat Rhythm

It has been found expedient to adopt the combination of (*a*) a semi-quaver, followed by a dotted quaver, with the beat falling on the semi-quaver, or

72

(*b*) a dotted quaver, followed by a semi-quaver, with the beat falling on the dotted quaver, as half-beats when counting steps or movements to music. Although neither of these combinations gives the sound of half-beats in a strict musical sense, since they are of unequal value, the semi-quaver being a quarter of a single beat, and the dotted quaver three quarters of a single beat, the time-value of either of the combinations still equals the time-value of one complete single beat.

Method (a)

The beat falling on the semi-quaver is frequently found in music for Highland Dancing, the counting being denoted as follows :

Method (b)

The beat falling on the dotted quaver is only occasionally found in music for Highland Dancing, the counting being denoted as follows :

Triple Beat Rhythm

Gives three sounds of equal value in the space of time occupied by a single beat. Thus there are twelve triple beats in the bar (represented by twelve quavers grouped in threes, with that number depicted above each group) and counted :

1 and a 2 and a 3 and a 4 and a

Note.—In the dances described in this book, Triple Beat Rhythm is not used in the counting of steps or movements to music, but it is widely used in other branches of dancing, good examples being the Irish Jig and Sailors' Hornpipe, which dances are frequently included at games or competitions.

Quadruple (or Quarter) Beat Rhythm

Gives four sounds of equal value in the space of time occupied by a single beat. Thus there are sixteen quadruple (or quarter) beats in the bar (each represented by a semi-quaver) and counted :

1 and and a 2 and and a 3 and and a 4 and and a

73

Note.—When an ' and ' is shown in brackets, this signifies that there is no action by the dancer on that quarter beat, nor should it be sounded when counting.

NOTES

1 When denoting Triple Beat Rhythm or Quadruple Beat Rhythm, the writer deems it advisable to use the word ' and ' fully written so that those rhythms may be quickly distinguished from Half-beat Rhythm and Imperfect Half-beat Rhythm, in both of which the ampersand ' & ' is invariably used.

2 Two consecutive bars of music may be grouped together for the purpose of counting a step or movement, in which case the counting for those two bars—in single beats—would be 1, 2, 3, 4, 5, 6, 7, 8.

3 In any movement, when two actions are executed almost simultaneously (for example a ' Spring Point '), these actions are counted as if they were executed simultaneously, i.e. to one count.

4 When executing any movement of elevation, the dancer should land on the count, except where otherwise stated.

5 When the working foot has to be placed in or raised to any specified position while executing a movement of elevation, that foot arrives at the specified position simultaneously with the dancer landing on the supporting foot unless otherwise stated.

6 Although Reel tunes are usually written in Common Time, they are played at a tempo so much faster than Strathspey tunes that it is found expedient to count steps or movements executed to Reel tunes as if the music were written in $\frac{2}{4}$ Time, that is to say, counting two in the bar so that crotchets count as half-beats and minims as single beats. Consequently, for the same movements or steps, we get the same counting, no matter whether that movement or step is executed to Strathspey Tempo or Reel Tempo. For example, the counting for a Pas de Basque is 1 & 2, 3 & 4 whether that movement is danced to Strathspey Tempo or to Reel Tempo, yet that Pas de Basque occupies only half a bar when danced to Strathspey Tempo and a complete bar when danced to Reel Tempo.

Chapter Four

COMPETITIONS

The rules and conditions recommended for competitions set forth in this chapter are those which have been adopted by the Scottish Official Board of Highland Dancing.

§ A RULES AND CONDITIONS

1 CHAMPIONSHIPS

(a) A Championship must be a competition to discover the best all-round dancer in the following traditional Highland Dances :

Highland Fling

Seann Triubhas

Sword Dance (Gillie Chaluim)

Strathspey or Reel of Tulloch ; or Strathspey and Highland Reel and Reel of Tulloch ; or Strathspey and Highland Reel or Reel of Tulloch

(b) No competition in Highland Dancing may be entitled ' Championship ' without the sanction of the Board.

(c) Championships must be held under the Scottish Official Board of Highland Dancing rules and must be advertised as ' Recognised by the S.O.B.H.D.'

2 TITLES OF CHAMPIONSHIPS

Titles of Championships are limited to the following four classes :

WORLD—Traditionally held at the Cowal Games.

NATIONAL—Covering a whole country or more.

AREA—Covering a large geographical area of a country, such as North, South, West or Midlands. In this case the boundaries of such areas must coincide with county boundaries. The boundaries of the proposed Area Championship must be clearly defined by the organisers and must receive the approval of the Board.

COUNTY—Covering one geographical county. The Board may sanction two adjacent counties holding one combined Championship, e.g. Sutherland and Caithness.

3 OPEN AND CLOSED CHAMPIONSHIPS

(a) An Open Championship is one in which competitors resident outwith the area named in its title may compete. A Closed Championship is one in which the competitor must be qualified by birth or by residence twelve months immediately prior to the event in the county, area or country covered by the Championship.

(*b*) When a person is qualified to compete in two County Championships —one by birth and one by residence—such person may not compete during any one calendar year in both Championships but must make his or her choice. The choice shall also determine which Closed Area Championship such person is entitled to enter.

(*c*) National and Area Championships may be either open or closed at the discretion of the organisers. If both are sanctioned by the Board they must be organised as separate events.

(*d*) County Championships must be closed.

4   RECOGNITION OF CHAMPIONSHIPS

(*a*) Application to the Board for the recognition of a competition as a Championship must be made in writing to reach the Board not less than three calendar months prior to the date set for that competition and must designate the FULL NAME and DESCRIPTION of the organising party, and give the DATE, VENUE, CLASSIFICATION and TYPE (Open or Closed) of the proposed championship.

(*b*) Should the organising party desire to hold *more than one championship at the same venue* on the same date, the details of each championship applied for may be set forth in the one application.

(*c*) Every application must be accompanied by a REGISTRATION FEE of £1 1s. od. in respect of each championship applied for, but should the Board refuse the recognition of a championship applied for, the registration fee shall be returned.

(*d*) A championship sanctioned by the Board may be held ONCE ONLY in any one calendar year.

(*e*) When applying for the RENEWAL OF RECOGNITION of a championship, the organising party shall follow the same procedure as laid down in paras (*a*), (*b*) and (*c*) above.

5   UNRECOGNISED ' CHAMPIONSHIPS '

A competitor who has taken part in any so-called championship not recognised by the Board, or any person who has acted as judge at such an event, shall be ineligible to compete or adjudicate respectively in any recognised championship until given permission to do so by the Board. Such permission may be withheld for so long as the Board may decide.

6   COMPETITIONS OTHER THAN CHAMPIONSHIPS

If a competition other than a championship is to be conducted according to the rules recommended by the S.O.B.H.D. the promoter shall be entitled to advertise to that effect.

7   JUDGING

(a) The judges for a championship must be selected from the Panel of Judges appointed annually by the Board. Failure to carry out this condition, unless a satisfactory explanation be given, shall nullify the event and jeopardise the renewal of recognition.

(b) At any championship, unless otherwise sanctioned by the Board, there must be at least three judges who shall mark independently. If for any unforeseen reason an appointed judge is unable to officiate, and if it is impossible to fill his place with an eligible judge, the remaining judges shall act, and the circumstances shall be announced to the competitors prior to the competition, and an explanation sent to the Board.

(c) A professional who acts as a judge at a professional championship is thereafter debarred from competing in a professional championship.

8   DEFINITION AND RIGHTS OF AN AMATEUR

(i) An Amateur is one who :

(a) Has never been employed or engaged or accepted remuneration, either in money or kind, as a dancer, a teacher of dancing, or an assistant to a teacher of dancing, or as an organiser or judge of competitions for personal profit.

(b) Has never taken part in a competition for which a money prize is offered (see para. ii (a)), or in connexion with which expenses of any kind are paid to competitors, excepting such expenses as are sanctioned by the Board and described in para. ii (b).

(c) Has never sold or converted into money a prize won for dancing.

(d) Has never declared himself or herself to be professional by advertisement or otherwise. Participation in a competition or match limited to professionals shall be taken as such a declaration. The passing of the entrance examination to any Branch of a Dance Teachers' Association or the taking of any examination confined to dance professionals shall be regarded as a definite act of professionalism.

(ii) Amateurs have the following rights :

(a) They are permitted to participate in mixed and general competitions for which money prizes are given to professionals provided an amateur receives no money as a prize and provided it is declared in the conditions of the competition that, in the event of an amateur winning a prize, such prize will not include any money.

(*b*) In the event of an amateur accepting an invitation to compete in a competition to be held in a town other than that in which he or she resides, then such amateur shall be allowed to accept the following expenses from the organiser of that competition :

(i) Bare travelling expenses from the town in which the amateur resides, to and from the town in which the competition is being held.

(ii) Bare hotel expenses incurred in the town in which the competition is being held, limited to the day or days of the competition and to one day before and one day after.

Note.—The above expenses must be in reimbursement of actual expenses personally incurred by the amateur in respect of himself or herself only.

9 OBJECTIONS

An objection to a person's eligibility to compete in any particular competition shall not be considered unless the complainant gives his or her full name and address accompanied by a deposit of £1 1s. od., which shall be returned should the objection be sustained. Such objection, unless admitted by the person complained against, shall be referred to the Board, but if there is not time to reach a decision before the event the person complained about shall be permitted to dance in the competition on the understanding that any award he or she may win shall be withheld until the decision of the Board be known. Should the objection be sustained those awards shall be passed down to the competitor next in order of merit and other awards suitably adjusted.

10 CERTIFICATES

The winner of a recognised Championship shall be entitled to a certificate issued by the Board and signed by the Chairman of the Board and the organising party or a representative of such. The second, third and (in certain cases) fourth prize winners may also be entitled to a certificate.

The organising party is responsible for :

(*a*) Providing the Board, within seven days of the event, with full particulars with which to complete the certificates.

(*b*) Forwarding the completed certificates to the winners as soon as possible and not later than two months from the holding of the competition.

11 GENERAL

Should any point arise not covered in the foregoing Rules and Conditions it shall be referred to the Board, whose decision shall be final.

§ B RECOMMENDATIONS

1 ACCOMMODATION AND MARSHALLING OF COMPETITORS

(*a*) Suitable changing and toilet accommodation should be provided for competitors.

(*b*) An official should be appointed for the purpose of marshalling competitors.

2 SIZE OF PLATFORM

The minimum dimensions of the dancing platform should be as follows :

Breadth	24 feet
Depth	18 feet
Height	$2\frac{1}{2}$ feet

3 EQUIPMENT

Highland Broadswords should invariably be used for the Sword Dance (Gillie Chaluim) and the organising party should endeavour to provide a sufficient number of such, i.e. for three dancers per platform.

No medals may be worn by competitors prior to the conclusion of the judging of any championship.

4 MAXIMUM NUMBER OF DANCERS ON PLATFORM

Highland Fling	Heats—4	Finals—4 (recommended 2 only)
Sword Dance	Heats—3	Finals—3 (recommended 2 only)
Seann Triubhas	Heats—3	Finals—3 (recommended 2 only)
Strathspey and/or Reel	Heats and Finals—one set only (4 dancers)	

5 SEQUENCE OF STEPS

The Board strongly recommends that in each dance at a competition the competitors should all dance the same steps in the same sequence. This would not only materially assist the judges in arriving at a decision, but would look better from the spectator's point of view. The steps in each dance are named and numbered in Chapter Two of this book, and the organising party should, in good time prior to the event, nominate the steps that are to be performed. When nominating the steps, the organising party should endeavour to include one or two different steps in each dance each year. Thus competitors would require to keep themselves conversant with all steps recognised by the Board and none of those steps would be liable to fall into disuse.

It should be borne in mind that (the last step of the Seann Triubhas excepted) the recognised first and last steps in each dance, as described in Chapter Two, must be retained as such.

6 POSITION OF JUDGES

In order to ensure independent decisions, judges should be so placed that, whilst having an uninterrupted view of the competitors, they are unable to communicate with each other by any means whilst judging is in progress.

During a competition, from the time the first heat begins until the final has been danced, no person shall be allowed to contact the judges except the scrutineer or the steward authorised to collect the judges' marking sheets on behalf of the scrutineer.

If, in order to make up the requisite number for a set in a Strathspey, Highland Reel, or Reel of Tulloch, it is necessary for a competitor to dance twice (or oftener) in the same heat, semi-final or final, such competitor shall be judged on his or her first appearance before the judges in that heat, semi-final or final.

7 JUDGES' MARKINGS

In each dance there shall be a maximum of 100 marks which shall be awarded under the following three headings :

Timing	Maximum marks—25
Technique	Maximum marks—50
General Deportment	Maximum marks—25

Timing—The ability of the dancer to keep good time to the music, particularly with regard to footwork.

Technique—Correct execution incorporating footwork in conjunction with head, arm and hand movement.

General Deportment—This covers ' interpretation ' (the ability of the dancer to express the spirit and motif of the dance), ' balance ', ' general appearance ' and ' comportment ', thus embracing carriage of the head, body, arms and hands.

The following specimen judge's card and scrutineering sheet are recommended :

JUDGE'S CARD

Title of Dance :   Place............................

....   Date ....

Class............   Section............   Dance..................... Judge...............

Competitors No.	Timing 25	Technique 50	General Deportment 25	Total 100

SCRUTINEERING SHEET

Title of Championship :   Place ....

....   Date ....

Class....................   Section.................   Dance............................

Competitors No.	Judge			Total	Result
	A	B	C		

81

§ C. AIDS TO JUDGES

If, in the opinion of a judge, the standard of dancing shown by a competitor is so much below average that such competitor stands no chance of being placed, the judge need not award marks to that competitor.

The technique compiled by the Board is the result of embodying what is considered to be the best of many styles, yet it allows an appreciable variation in the method of presentation and considerable scope for individual interpretation. Therefore, provided a competitor conforms to that technique, judges must not allow personal stylistic preference to bias their judgment.

Timing

(*a*) Refers to correct timing of arm movements as well as those of feet.

(*b*) If a competitor dances ' off the beat ' throughout a dance, no marks should be awarded to such competitor in that dance for Timing but, should a competitor begin a dance ' off the beat ', then correct that fault, the competitor should be penalised by loss of marks as assessed by the judge.

Technique

Footwork demands the correct placing of the feet during the performance. The ability to apply the recognised ground and aerial foot positions is the foundation upon which all good dancing is built, so it is essential that they be closely adhered to throughout. No matter how superficially showy a movement may appear it is never really attractive if performed ' out of position '. Judges should bear in mind that the supporting foot should be as closely watched as the working foot.

In the Sword Dance, five marks should be deducted from a competitor every time he or she touches the swords without displacing them, but should a competitor touch and thereby displace the swords, he or she shall be disqualified in that dance.

General Deportment should show :

(*a*) Pleasure in the dance.

(*b*) Supple movement with lack of strain.

(*c*) Upright carriage.

(*d*) Freedom from elaborate ' showiness '.

(*e*) Apparent ' unhurriedness ' in dancing.

(*f*) Buoyancy without exaggerated elevation.

Chapter Five

DRESS FOR HIGHLAND DANCERS

(*As recommended by the Board*)

The recognised forms of dress for male Highland dancers have not altered appreciably in use and practice during the last century, and little requires to be said about them. However, a general description will not go amiss.

MALES

TYPE 1

Jacket—May be of velvet or cloth in any colour and any recognised style of doublet or coatee. Garments are generally, but not always, worn with a dirk belt with which a dirk may or may not be used at the discretion of the wearer.

Kilt—Any clan or family tartan.

Sporran—Evening pattern, usually sealskin with plated metal top. Hair full dress sporran is *not* correct for competitive dancers.

Stockings—Tartan, to match kilt.

Garter flashes—Red or green.

Head dress—Balmoral or glengarry bonnet, with appropriate crest. The clan badge may be worn behind the crest. Feathers should not be worn.

Skean dhu—Worn if desired.

Footwear—Black Highland dancing pumps.

Plaid—Belted plaid may be worn at the discretion of the dancer.

Jabot—In lace, or a black bow tie are optional.

Ruffles—Optional if jabot is worn and must be attached to the sleeve of the shirt or coat.

TYPE 2

Jacket and waistcoat—Day wear style, in Lovat or other type of tweed.

Kilt—Any clan or family tartan.

Sporran—Leather, any pattern.

Stockings—Plain to tone with jacket, or marl leg with tartan top.

Skean dhu—Worn if desired.

Footwear—Black Highland dancing pumps.

TYPE 3

The outfit as in Type 2 may be worn without the jacket and waistcoat, and with a white shirt and tartan or other tie.

FEMALES

The dress for female Highland dancers may consist only of skirt and white blouse, but a jacket or a waistcoat may be worn over the blouse. The legs may be bare or hose may be worn.

Skirt—Kilt reaching to the centre of the knee.

White blouse—Full or half-length sleeves as desired, with a lace-ornamented front and a lace stand at the back of the neck. The lace stand is an upright stiffened lace half-collar, approximately $1\frac{1}{4}$ in. in depth, attached to the blouse.

Jacket—Black or coloured velvet with no outside pockets, close fitting at the waist and hips, and fastened only at the waist, the basque having two points in front and wide scallops. The jacket is trimmed round the edges with a single row of $\frac{1}{2}$ in. silver braid. The facings have a single row of not more than five ornamental buttons on each side. The full length sleeves may have a single row of not more than five silver buttons at the vent. If desired, ruffles (not exceeding 1 in. in depth) may be worn at the wrist, but they must be fastened to the sleeve.

Waistcoat—Similar to the jacket as described above, but without sleeves, there being no trimming round the armholes.

Hose—If worn, may be (*a*) full tartan ; (*b*) marl leg with a tartan top ; or (*c*) long hose.

Footwear—Black Highland dancing pumps.

Underwear—Dark or tartan trews should be worn.

Note.—The front edges of the jacket are boned from the waist up and elastic loops are fitted inside to fasten to the top of the kilt in order to prevent the jacket from rising when the arms are raised.

The following items should *not* be worn :

Skean dhu	Plaid	Bows
Sporran	Flashes	Other ornaments of
Belt	Bonnet	any description

Printed in Great Britain by
Thomas Nelson and Sons Ltd, Edinburgh